Financial & Managerial Accounting, 6e

OR

Managerial Accounting, 6e

Warren • Reeve • Fess

Prepared by

James M. Reeve
University of Tennessee, Knoxville

Carl S. Warren
University of Georgia, Athens

 South-Western College Publishing
an International Thomson Publishing company I(T)P®

Cincinnati · Albany · Boston · Detroit · Johannesburg · London · Madrid · Melbourne · Mexico City
New York · Pacific Grove · San Francisco · Scottsdale · Singapore · Tokyo · Toronto

Accounting Team Director: Richard Lindgren
Senior Acquisitions Editor: David L. Shaut
Senior Marketing Manager: Sharon Oblinger
Senior Developmental Editor: Ken Martin
Production Editor: Mark Sears
Production Services: Mary A. Hartkemeyer

International Thomson Publishing
South-Western is an ITP Company. The ITP trademark is used under license.

ISBN: 0-538-87363-9

    3 4 5 6 7   MZ   4 3 2 1 0 9

Printed in the United States of America

Contents

14

Introduction to Managerial Accounting and Job Order Cost Systems

QUIZ AND TEST HINTS

The following hints may be helpful to you in preparing for a quiz or a test over the material covered in Chapter 14.

1. This chapter introduces managerial accounting concepts and terminology. Instructors normally test this material using true/false and multiple-choice questions. As a review of the key terms, do the Matching Exercise on pages 658–659.

2. It is important to be able to distinguish between direct and indirect materials, labor, and overhead; and between product and period costs.

3. You should be able to prepare journal entries for the recording of transactions using a job order cost system. Carefully review the chapter illustration of the job order cost system. Also, the Illustrative Problem on page 656 is a useful study aid.

4. You should be able to calculate factory overhead application rates using different activity bases.

FILL IN THE BLANK—Part A

Instructions: Answer the following questions or complete the statements by writing the appropriate words or amounts in the answer blanks.

1. _____ accounting information is prepared in accordance to generally accepted accounting principles for the use of government agencies, creditors, and public investors.

2. A(n) _____ department is one that provides services and assistance to other departments.

3. A(n) _____ is a payment of cash or its equivalent or the commitment to pay cash in the future for the purpose of generating revenues.

4. If a technician is directly involved in converting materials into finished products, his or her salary should be classified as a(n) _____ _____ cost.

5. Shark Company owns dozens of machines used on its product assembly line. Depreciation expenses for these assets should be classified as _____ _____ costs.

6. A company uses an electric furnace to melt iron ore. Costs of running the furnace, a necessary step in converting iron ore into steel, are known as factory overhead costs or _____ costs.

7. Beta Company manufactures customized fiber-optic systems for NASA's space missions. If separate records are kept for the cost of each individual product that the company produces, Beta's accountants are using a(n) _____ _____ cost system.

8. If 1,000 springs are moved out of the storeroom and into the assembly line, the company's accounting system will reflect this flow of materials by _____ the materials account and _____ the work in process account.

9. With a job order cost system, factory workers record the hours they spend working on specific jobs using forms known as _____ _____.

10. Cost _____ is the process of assigning factory overhead costs to a cost object, such as a job.

11. Amber Company estimates that its total factory overhead costs will amount to $75,000 this year. If the company operated its only machine for 1,800 hours this year, the predetermined factory overhead rate per hour of machine time is _____ (round your answer to the nearest whole dollar).

12. A new method of allocating factory overhead costs using different rates corresponding to different activities is known as _____-_____ costing.

13. If the factory overhead account has a credit balance at the end of the period, the credit is described as _____ overhead.

14. During one month, Smith Company had a beginning debit balance of $13,200 in its factory overhead account. By the end of the month, the account had increased 75%, ending with a debit balance of $23,100. The company's accountant should investigate the overhead _____ to determine whether it needs revision.

15. One approach for disposing of the balance of factory overhead at the end of the year is to transfer the entire balance to the _____ _____ _____ _____ account.

16. Direct materials costs are debited to Work in Process based on data obtained from a summary of _____ _____.

17. The finished goods account is a controlling account with a subsidiary ledger called a finished goods ledger or _____ _____.

18. Expenses that are not incurred to support the manufacturing process, and which are incurred during the current period of time, are called _____ costs.

19. _____ expenses are incurred in the administration of the business and are not related to the manufacturing or selling functions.

20. A job order cost system is useful for both manufacturing and _____ businesses.

FILL IN THE BLANK—Part B

Instructions: Answer the following questions or complete the statements by writing the appropriate words or amounts in the answer blanks.

1. _____ accounting information includes both historical and estimated data used by a company to conduct daily operations, plan future operations, and develop an overall business strategy.

2. If a department is directly involved in manufacturing activities, it is known as a(n) _____ department.

3. Another title for a firm's chief management accountant is the firm's _____.

4. Woods Company, a manufacturer of air compressors, regularly buys flow regulators from an outside vendor. If they are an integral component for the final product, flow regulators should be classified as _____ _____ costs.

5. Labor costs that do not enter directly into the manufacture of a product are classified as _____ _____ and are recorded as factory overhead.

6. Managerial accountants gather information related to product costs. Managers frequently use this information to establish _____ _____, control operations, and develop financial statements.

7. Each inventory account, including Raw Materials Inventory, Work in Process Inventory, and Finished Goods Inventory, is _____ for all additions and _____ for all deductions.

8. Materials are released from the storeroom to the factory in response to materials _____ received from the production department.

9. Under the job order cost system, a(n) _____ _____ sheet is used to keep track of the resources consumed during the production of a specific customer order.

10. A summary of the _____ _____ at the end of each month is the basis for recording the direct and indirect labor costs incurred in production.

11. The measure used to allocate factory overhead is frequently called an activity base, allocation base, or _____ _____.

12. Green Company has a predetermined factory overhead rate of $3.75 per direct labor hour. If Green Company uses 1,500 hours as the activity cost driver for direct labor, the estimated total factory overhead cost is _____.

13. Gold Company uses $4.00 per hour as a cost driver for allocating direct labor costs as factory overhead. If Job A requires a total of 16½ hours of direct labor, the amount of factory overhead to be applied to Job A is _____.

14. Factory overhead costs applied to production are periodically debited to the _____ _____ _____ account and credited to the factory overhead account.

15. If the factory overhead account has a debit balance at the end of the period, the debit is described as _____ overhead.

16. Direct labor and factory overhead costs are debited to Work in Process based on data obtained from a summary of _____ _____.

17. Each account in the _____ _____ ledger contains cost data including the units manufactured, units sold, and the units on hand for each of the individual product types which the company manufactures.

18. Randolph Company completed 20,000 units at a cost of $175,000. The beginning finished goods inventory was 3,500 units, costing a total of $26,600. The cost of goods sold for 12,000 units, assuming a fifo cost flow, is _____.

19. _____ expenses are incurred in marketing the product and delivering the sold product to customers.

20. The Silver Agency sells advertising services. When the agency completes a job and a client is billed, the accountant will transfer the job's costs from a work in process account to a(n) _____ _____ _____ account.

MULTIPLE CHOICE

Instructions: Circle the best answer for each of the following questions.

1. For which of the following businesses would the process cost system be most appropriate?
    a. building contractor
    b. cookie processor
    c. plumber
    d. textbook publisher

2. The production department requests that materials be released from the storeroom to the factory based on which of the following forms?
    a. receiving report
    b. purchase order
    c. purchase requisition
    d. materials requisition

3. The amount of time spent by each employee on an individual job is recorded on a(n):
    a. clock card
    b. time ticket
    c. in-and-out card
    d. labor requisition

4. For which of the following businesses would the job order cost system be most appropriate?
    a. oil refinery
    b. meat processor
    c. electrical utility
    d. textbook publisher

5. The subsidiary ledger that contains the individual accounts for each product produced is called the:
    a. work in process ledger
    b. finished goods ledger
    c. factory overhead ledger
    d. materials ledger

6. Which of the following would not be considered part of overhead costs?
    a. property taxes on factory building
    b. insurance on factory building
    c. sales salaries
    d. depreciation on factory plant and equipment

7. A characteristic of managerial accounting is:

    a. strict adherence to GAAP

    b. a focus on external decision maker needs

    c. a focus on management decision needs

    d. all of the above

8. The amount of actual factory overhead in excess of the factory overhead applied to production during a period is called:

    a. underapplied factory overhead

    b. excess factory overhead

    c. overapplied factory overhead

    d. excess capacity

9. A method of accumulating and allocating factory overhead costs to products using many overhead rates is:

    a. variable costing

    b. flexible costing

    c. activity-based costing

    d. service function allocation

10. Which of the following would be considered a staff position in a business organization?

    a. controller

    b. plant manager

    c. regional sales manager

    d. all of the above

TRUE/FALSE

Instructions: Indicate whether each of the following statements is true or false by placing a check mark in the appropriate column.

	True	False

1. A cost accounting system uses perpetual inventory procedures in accounting for manufacturing costs....................... _____ _____

2. A process cost system provides for a separate record of cost of each particular quantity of product that passes through the factory. .... _____ _____

3. A publishing company which produces a variety of different publication titles would normally use a process cost accounting system... _____ _____

4. The two principal types of cost systems for manufacturing operations are job order cost accounting and process cost accounting systems.. _____ _____

5. Materials are transferred from the storeroom to the factory in response to purchase requisitions..................................... _____ _____

6. As a practical matter, unless the total amount of the underapplied or overapplied overhead balance is large, it is transferred to Cost of Goods Sold... _____ _____

7. If the factory overhead account has a debit balance, the factory overhead is said to be overapplied........................... _____ _____

8. The subsidiary ledger that contains the individual accounts for each kind of product is the finished goods ledger........... _____ _____

9. A manufacturer that uses a job order cost system for one product must use that system for all products..................... _____ _____

10. The predetermined factory overhead rate is calculated by relating the estimated amount of factory overhead for the period to an activity base... _____ _____

EXERCISE 14-1

Instructions: Indicate the flow of costs through the perpetual inventory accounts and into the cost of goods sold account for a cost accounting system by connecting with arrows the letters that should be paired together in the following diagram.

Materials		Work in Process		Finished Goods	
Purchased	Dir. used a	e	Finished k	l	Sold m
	Indir. used b	f			
		g			

Wages Payable		Factory Overhead		Cost of Goods Sold	
Paid	Dir. used c	h	Applied j	n	
	Indir. used d	i			
		Other costs			

EXERCISE 14-2

Instructions: Indicate the flow of costs through a service business using a job order cost accounting system by connecting with arrows the letters that should be paired together in the following diagram.

Wages Payable		Work in Process		Cost of Services	
Paid	Dir. labor a	d	Completed	j	
	Indir. labor b	g	jobs i		

Supplies		Overhead			
Purchased	Used c	e	Applied h		
		f			
		Other costs			

EXERCISE 14-3

Foley Company operates two factories. It applies factory overhead to jobs on the basis of machine hours in Factory 1 and on the basis of direct labor costs in Factory 2. Estimated factory overhead costs, direct labor costs, and machine hours for the year and actual amounts for January are as follows:

	Factory 1	Factory 2
Estimated factory overhead cost for year	$65,000	$243,600
Estimated direct labor costs for year		$580,000
Estimated machine hours for year	20,000	
Actual factory overhead costs for January	$6,050	$20,100
Actual direct labor costs for January		$48,500
Actual machine hours for January	1,800	

Instructions

a. Determine the factory overhead rate for Factory 1. _____

b. Determine the factory overhead rate for Factory 2. _____

c. Journalize the entries to apply factory overhead to production in each factory for January.

JOURNAL

PAGE

	DATE	DESCRIPTION	POST. REF.	DEBIT	CREDIT	
1						1
2						2
3						3
4						4
5						5
6						6
7						7
8						8
9						9
10						10

d. Determine the balance of the factory overhead account in each factory as of January 31, and indicate whether the amounts represent overapplied or underapplied factory overhead.

PROBLEM 14-1

Instructions: Below are listed some transactions of Zintor Inc., which uses a job order cost accounting system. Prepare the entries to record the transactions. (Omit dates and explanations.)

(1) Purchased materials costing $60,000 and incurred prepaid expenses amounting to $5,300, all on account.

(2) Requisitioned $23,200 worth of materials to be used directly in production ($15,400 on Job 101 and $7,800 on Job 102) and $1,200 worth of materials to be used indirectly for repairs and maintenance.

(3) Factory labor used as follows: direct labor, $35,900; indirect labor, $2,700.

(4) Other costs incurred on account as follows: factory overhead, $12,200; selling expenses, $21,950; administrative expenses, $15,300. (Credit Accounts Payable.)

(5) Prepaid expenses expired as follows: factory overhead, $5,000; selling expenses, $800; administrative expenses, $600.

(6) The predetermined rate for the application of factory overhead to jobs (work in process) was 70% of direct labor cost. (See transaction 3.)

(7) The cost of jobs completed was $53,000.

(8) The sales on account for the period amounted to $160,000. The cost of goods sold was $110,000.

JOURNAL   PAGE

	DATE	DESCRIPTION	POST. REF.	DEBIT	CREDIT	
1						1
2						2
3						3
4						4
5						5
6						6
7						7
8						8
9						9
10						10
11						11
12						12
13						13
14						14
15						15
16						16
17						17

JOURNAL   PAGE _____

	DATE		DESCRIPTION	POST. REF.	DEBIT	CREDIT	
1							1
2							2
3							3
4							4
5							5
6							6
7							7
8							8
9							9
10							10
11							11
12							12
13							13
14							14
15							15
16							16
17							17
18							18
19							19
20							20
21							21
22							22
23							23
24							24
25							25
26							26
27							27
28							28
29							29
30							30
31							31
32							32
33							33
34							34
35							35
36							36

PROBLEM 14-2

Instructions: Post the following transactions to the proper T accounts below. Identify the postings with the transactions by using the number preceding each transaction.

(1) Purchased materials for $78,000 cash.

(2) Requisitioned $56,000 worth of direct materials and $2,400 worth of indirect materials from the storeroom.

(3) The factory labor cost for the period amounted to $75,000. (Credit Wages Payable.) The labor cost is determined to be $70,000 direct labor, $5,000 indirect labor.

(4) Paid $12,500 for factory overhead costs.

(5) Applied $24,000 of factory overhead to work in process.

(6) The cost of jobs completed amounted to $164,000.

Cash		Finished Goods	
Bal. 135,400		Bal. 50,800	

Work in Process		Materials	
Bal. 33,800		Bal. 18,000	

Factory Overhead		Wages Payable	
Bal. 3,000			

15

Process Cost Systems

QUIZ AND TEST HINTS

The following hints may be helpful to you in preparing for a quiz or a test over the material covered in Chapter 15.

1. The focus of this chapter is accounting for manufacturing operations using a process cost system. You can expect to see at least one problem requiring you to prepare journal entries for process costing or a cost of production report. The illustration of process costing in the chapter and the Illustrative Problem are good study aids.

2. You have to be able to compute equivalent units of production and cost per equivalent unit. In addition to a problem requiring the preparation of a cost of production report, expect to see some multiple-choice questions requiring equivalent unit computations.

3. Terminology is important. Study the highlighted terms in the chapter for possible true/false or multiple-choice questions. As a review of the key terms, do the Matching Exercise on page 699.

FILL IN THE BLANK—Part A

Instructions: Answer the following questions or complete the statements by writing the appropriate words or amounts in the answer blanks.

1. A _____ (specify process or job order) cost system would be more appropriate for a shipbuilding company.

2. A _____ (specify process or job order) cost system would be more appropriate for an oil refining company.

3. Direct materials, direct labor, and _____ _____ are the three elements of product costs.

4. In a process cost system, the amount of work in process inventory is determined by _____ costs between completed and partially completed units within a department.

5. In a process cost system, product cost flows should reflect the _____ flow of materials passing through the manufacturing process.

6. Smith Company refines oil. If the company sells 5,000 gallons of oil, should the finished goods account be debited or credited? _____

7. The first step in determining the cost of goods completed and the ending inventory valuation is to determine the _____ _____ _____ _____ _____ .

8. Omega Department had a beginning in-process inventory of 24,000 pounds. During the month, 58,500 pounds were completed and transferred to another department. The ending in-process inventory was 16,000 pounds. During the period, _____ pounds were started and completed.

9. The number of units that could have been completed during a given accounting period is called the _____ units of production.

10–13. Department G had 8,000 units in work in process that were 40% converted at the beginning of the period at a cost of $19,450. During the period, 18,000 units of direct materials were added at a cost of $54,000, 18,500 units were completed, and 7,500 units were 40% completed. Direct labor was $32,500, and factory overhead was $66,320 during the period.

10. The number of conversion equivalent units was _____ .

11. The total conversion costs were _____ .

12. The conversion costs of the units started and completed during the period were _____ .

13. The conversion costs of the 7,500 units in process at the end of the period were _____ .

14. The _____ _____ _____ _____ is determined by dividing the direct materials and conversion costs by the respective total equivalent units for direct materials and conversion costs.

15. The oxidation department had $68,000 of direct materials cost and 128 direct materials equivalent units. The cost per equivalent unit of direct materials is _____.

16. Department Z had $99,510 of conversion costs and $5.35 of cost per equivalent unit of conversion. The number of conversion equivalent units is _____.

17. The _____ _____ _____ report summarizes (1) the units for which the department is accountable and their disposition, and (2) the costs charged to the department and their allocation.

18. The ratio of the materials output quantity to the materials input quantity is known as the _____.

19. A production philosophy focused on reducing production time and costs and eliminating poor quality is known as _____-_____-_____ processing.

20. Separate process functions combined into "work centers" are sometimes called _____ _____.

FILL IN THE BLANK—Part B

Instructions: Answer the following questions or complete the statements by writing the appropriate words or amounts in the answer blanks.

1. A _____ (specify process or job order) cost system would be more appropriate for a company that continually produces a homogenous product.

2. A _____ (specify process or job order) cost system would be more appropriate for a company that builds specialized products according to individual contracts with its customers.

3. In a process cost system, product costs are accumulated by _____.

4. The two elements of conversion costs are _____ _____ and _____ _____.

5. Costs transferred from one department to another normally include direct materials and _____ costs.

6. When the first units entering a production process are the first to be completed, the flow of production would be described as a(n) _____ flow.

7. The last step in determining the cost of goods completed and the ending inventory valuation is "to allocate costs to transferred and _____ _____ units."

8. The three categories of units to be assigned costs for an accounting period are (1) units in beginning in-process inventory, (2) units started and completed during the period, and (3) units in _____ _____-_____ _____.

9. This month, Alpha Department had 100 units in beginning in-process inventory that were completed during the month, 300 units started and completed, and 200 units in ending in-process inventory. In order to reflect this month's activity, _____ total units should be assigned costs.

10. The number of units in production during a period, regardless of whether they are completed or not, is called the _____ units of production.

11. On April 1, Department X had a beginning in-process inventory of 300 gallons of a special chemical. The 300 gallons should be counted as equivalent units of direct materials for the month of _____.

12. Conversion costs are usually incurred _____ throughout a process.

13. Department B had a beginning work in process inventory of 200 half-finished assemblies. This month the department completed 550 assemblies, leaving 120 half-finished assemblies in ending work in process inventory. The equivalent units for conversion costs are _____.

14. Echo Department had $25,000 in conversion costs and 1,000 conversion equivalent units. The cost per equivalent unit of conversion is _____.

15. Department 2 had $55,000 of conversion costs and $6.25 of cost per equivalent unit of conversion. The number of conversion equivalent units is _____.

16. The cost of transferred and partially completed units is calculated by _____ equivalent unit rates by the number of equivalent units.

17–19. A department calculated that it had 600 equivalent units for direct materials and 300 equivalent units for conversion in this month's ending inventory. Equivalent cost per unit of direct materials was $17.25, and equivalent cost per unit of conversion was $5.30.

17. The cost of direct materials in ending inventory is _____.

18. The cost of conversion in ending inventory is _____.

19. The total cost of ending inventory is _____.

20. In a JIT system, each work center may be connected to the other work centers through information contained on _____, which is a Japanese term for cards.

MULTIPLE CHOICE

Instructions: Circle the best answer for each of the following questions.

1. In the manufacture of 10,000 equivalent units of product for a period, direct materials cost incurred was $200,000, direct labor cost incurred was $75,000, and applied factory overhead cost was $185,000. What was the unit conversion cost for the period?

   a. $7.50

   b. $18.50

   c. $26

   d. $46

2. The Finishing Department had 6,000 units, 1/3 completed at the beginning of the period; 16,000 units were transferred to the Finishing Department from the Sanding Department during the period; and 2,500 units were 1/5 completed at the end of the period. What is the total units to be accounted for on the cost of production report for the Finishing Department for the period?

   a. 13,500

   b. 15,500

   c. 18,500

   d. 22,000

3. Material B is added after the processing is 60% completed. There were 2,400 units completed during the period. There were 300 units in beginning inventory (50% completed) and 100 units in process at the end of the period (20% completed). What was the total equivalent units of production for Material B?

   a. 2,400

   b. 2,200

   c. 2,500

   d. 2,700

4. If the Weaving Department had 900 units, 40% completed, in process at the beginning of the period; 9,000 units were completed during the period; and 600 units were 10% completed at the end of the period, what was the number of conversion equivalent units of production for the period using the fifo cost method?

   a. 8,520

   b. 8,700

   c. 8,900

   d. 9,060

5. The number of units that could have been completed within a given accounting period is called the:

   a. equivalent units of production

   b. optimal units of production

   c. theoretical units of production

   d. processing capacity

6. The combined direct labor and factory overhead per equivalent unit is called the:

   a. prime cost per unit

   b. processing cost per unit

   c. conversion cost per unit

   d. combined cost per unit

7. The ratio of the materials output quantity to the materials input quantity is the:

   a. materials consumption ratio

   b. materials absorption ratio

   c. capacity constraint

   d. yield

8. Cards that contain information to help work centers communicate with one another in a just-in-time processing system are called:

   a. pillars

   b. kanbans

   c. JIT cards

   d. flow cards

9. Work centers in a just-in-time processing system where processing functions are combined are:

   a. JIT centers

   b. combined processing centers

   c. master cells

   d. manufacturing cells

10. There were 2,000 pounds in process at the beginning of the period in the Finishing Department. The department received 22,000 pounds from the Blending Department during the period, and 3,000 pounds were in process at the end of the period. How many pounds were completed by the Finishing Department during the period?

    a. 27,000

    b. 24,000

    c. 21,000

    d. 19,000

TRUE/FALSE

Instructions: Indicate whether each of the following statements is true or false by placing a check mark in the appropriate column.

	True	**False**

1. The number of units that could have been completed within a given accounting period is referred to as the equivalent units of production... ____ ____

2. A report prepared periodically for each processing department and which summarizes (a) the units for which the department is accountable and the disposition of those units and (b) the production costs incurred by the department and the allocation of those costs is called a cost of production report. .... ____ ____

3. The accumulated costs transferred from preceding departments and the costs of direct materials and direct labor incurred in each processing department are debited to the related work in process accounts.. ____ ____

4. The most important use of the cost of production report is to schedule production. .... ____ ____

5. Direct labor and factory overhead are referred to as primary costs. .... ____ ____

6. Equivalent units for materials and conversion costs are usually determined separately. .... ____ ____

7. A cost of production report will normally list costs in greater detail to help management isolate problems and opportunities... ____ ____

8. If a material is introduced halfway through processing and the beginning inventory is 40% complete, then the equivalent units for beginning inventory for this material will be zero (assuming fifo)... ____ ____

9. The first-in, first-out cost method is based on the assumption that the work in process at the beginning of the current period was started and completed during the current period... ____ ____

10. If the work in process at the beginning of the period is 400 gallons, 1,600 gallons were started during the period, and 300 gallons remained in process at the end of the period, then the units started and completed are 1,700 gallons. ..... ____ ____

EXERCISE 15-1

Instructions: Presented below is a diagram of the cost flows for Cortex Company, a process manufacturer. Cortex has two processing departments. All materials are placed into production in Department 1. In the spaces beneath the diagram identify each letter contained in the diagram.

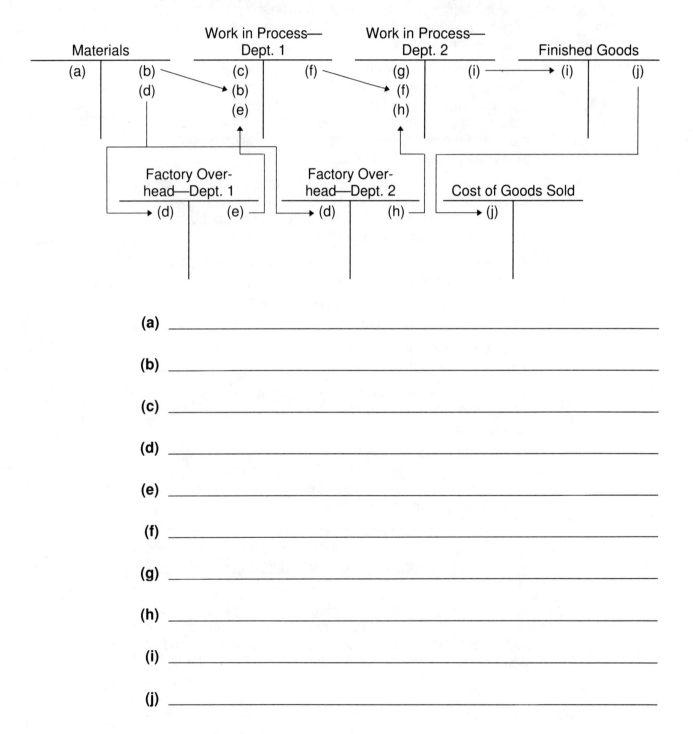

(a) _____

(b) _____

(c) _____

(d) _____

(e) _____

(f) _____

(g) _____

(h) _____

(i) _____

(j) _____

EXERCISE 15-2

Ellis Company started April with 12,000 units in process that were 30% complete at a cost of $32,600. During April, the following costs were incurred: direct materials, $148,800; direct labor, $141,000; and factory overhead, $185,400. During April, 66,000 units were completed and transferred to finished goods. There were 8,000 units in process that were 20% completed at April 30. All materials are added at the beginning of the production process and conversion costs are incurred evenly throughout.

Instructions: Use the work sheet presented below to determine the following:

(1) Equivalent units of production for materials costs .... _____

(2) Equivalent units of production for conversion costs .... _____

(3) Materials cost per equivalent unit .... $ _____

(4) Conversion cost per equivalent unit .... $ _____

(5) Work in process inventory, April 30 .... $ _____

(6) Cost of goods transferred to finished goods warehouse .. $ _____

Units	Total Whole Units	% Material to be Completed in April	% Conversion to be Completed in April	(1) Equivalent Units for Materials	(2) Equivalent Units for Conversion

Costs	(3) Direct Materials	(4) Conversion Costs	Total
(6)			
(5)			

PROBLEM 15-1

Mirror Inc. is a small manufacturing company that uses a process cost accounting system. The firm has two processing departments.

Instructions: Record the following transactions in the journals provided. Any indirect cost such as indirect labor or indirect material incurred by a department should be charged to the department's overhead account. (Omit dates and explanations.)

(1)   Materials purchased on account, $210,000.

(2)   The following materials were requisitioned: Department 10, direct, $18,000; Department 10, indirect, $2,100; Department 20, direct, $24,000; Department 20, indirect, $600.

(3)   The labor used by factory departments was as follows: Department 10, direct, $25,000; Department 10, indirect, $2,700; Department 20, direct, $20,000; Department 20, indirect, $2,700.

(4)   The following other costs and expenses were incurred on account: factory overhead, Department 10, $1,500; factory overhead, Department 20, $2,250.

(5)   Depreciation expenses were as follows: Department 10, $4,200; Department 20, $3,150.

(6)   Factory overhead costs were applied to work in process on the basis of 102% of the direct labor cost of Department 10 and 75% of the direct labor cost of Department 20. (See transaction 3.)

(7)   There was no beginning or ending inventory in Department 10. All costs accumulated in Department 10 work in process were transferred to Department 20.

(8)   The work in process in Department 20 at the end of the period amounted to $12,500. The balance (representing 20,000 units) was transferred to finished goods. (There was no beginning inventory of work in process.)

(9)   Sales of 21,000 units for $160,000 on account were made during the month. The cost of goods sold was $122,000.

JOURNAL PAGE _____

	DATE		DESCRIPTION	POST. REF.	DEBIT	CREDIT	
1							1
2							2
3							3
4							4
5							5
6							6
7							7
8							8
9							9
10							10
11							11
12							12
13							13
14							14
15							15
16							16
17							17
18							18
19							19
20							20
21							21
22							22
23							23
24							24
25							25
26							26
27							27
28							28
29							29
30							30
31							31
32							32
33							33
34							34
35							35
36							36

JOURNAL   PAGE

	DATE	DESCRIPTION	POST. REF.	DEBIT	CREDIT	
1						1
2						2
3						3
4						4
5						5
6						6
7						7
8						8
9						9
10						10
11						11
12						12
13						13
14						14
15						15
16						16
17						17
18						18
19						19
20						20
21						21
22						22
23						23
24						24
25						25

PROBLEM 15-2

Instructions: Prepare a cost of production report for the Polishing Department of Ivy Inc. for March of the current fiscal year using the fifo cost method and the following data:

Inventory, March 1, 5,000 units, 30% completed	$ 37,025
Materials from the Cutting Department, 21,000 units	105,000
Direct labor for March	176,140
Factory overhead for March	120,000
Inventory, March 31, 6,000 units, 60% completed	——

Ivy Inc.

Cost of Production Report—Polishing Department

For the Month Ended March 31, 20--

UNITS	WHOLE UNITS	EQUIVALENT UNITS	
		DIRECT MATERIALS	CONVERSION

Ivy Inc.

Cost of Production Report—Polishing Department (Concluded)

For the Month Ended March 31, 20--

COSTS	COSTS		
	DIRECT MATERIALS	CONVERSION	TOTAL COSTS

16

Cost Behavior and Cost-Volume-Profit Analysis

QUIZ AND TEST HINTS

The following hints may be helpful to you in preparing for a quiz or a test over the material covered in Chapter 16.

1. Many new terms are introduced in this chapter. You can expect true/false, multiple-choice, or matching questions testing your knowledge of these terms. As a review of the key terms, do the Matching Exercise on page 739.

2. Expect some multiple-choice questions related to the behavior of costs. For example, you might be required to classify various types of costs (direct materials, for example) as variable, fixed, or mixed for the activity of units produced. You might also have to use the high-low method to separate a mixed cost into its variable and fixed costs components.

3. The major focus of this chapter is the computation of break-even sales (units) and sales (units) required to achieve a target profit. These computations are based upon the contribution margin concept. In your studying, focus on the mathematical approach to cost-volume-profit analysis. Instructors often do not require preparation of a cost-volume-profit or a profit-volume chart.

4. The special cost-volume-profit relationships (margin of safety and operating leverage) and the assumptions of cost-volume-profit analysis often appear in the form of true/false or multiple-choice questions on tests.

FILL IN THE BLANK—Part A

Instructions: Answer the following questions or complete the statements by writing the appropriate words or amounts in the answer blanks.

1. Activities that are thought to cause a cost to be incurred are called _____ _____.

2. The range of activity over which the changes in a cost are of interest to management is referred to as the _____ _____.

3. In terms of cost behavior, direct materials and labor costs are generally classified as _____ _____.

4. Straight-line depreciation of factory equipment and insurance on factory plant are examples of _____ (variable, fixed, or mixed) costs.

5. Rental of equipment at $2,000 per month plus $1 for each machine hour used over 10,000 hours is a type of _____ (variable, fixed, or mixed) cost.

6. The high-low method is a cost estimate technique that may be used to separate _____ (variable, fixed, or mixed) costs.

7. A management accounting reporting system that includes only variable manufacturing costs in the product cost is known as variable costing or _____ _____.

8. _____-_____-_____ analysis is the systematic examination of the relationship among selling prices, sales and production volume, costs, expenses, and profits.

9. Sales minus variable costs divided by sales is the calculation of the _____ _____ _____.

10. Given a selling price per unit of $20, variable costs per unit of $10, and fixed costs of $95,000, the break-even point in sales units is _____.

11. An increase in fixed costs will cause the break-even point to _____.

12. Increases in the price of direct materials and the wages of factory workers will cause the break-even point to _____.

13. If fixed costs are $200,000 and the unit contribution margin is $40, the sales volume in units needed to earn a target profit of $100,000 is _____.

14. A cost-volume-profit chart is also called a(n) _____-_____ chart.

15. On a cost-volume-profit chart, units of sales are plotted along the _____ axis.

16. The _____-_____ chart is a graphic approach to cost-volume-profit analysis that focuses on profits.

17. With computers, managers can vary assumptions regarding selling prices, costs, and volume and can see immediately the effects on the break-even point. This is known as _____ _____ _____.

18. The relative distribution of sales among the various products sold by a business is called the _____ _____.

19. The difference between the current sales revenue and the sales at the break-even point is called the _____ _____ _____.

20. _____ _____ is computed by dividing the contribution margin by the operating income.

FILL IN THE BLANK—Part B

Instructions: Answer the following questions or complete the statements by writing the appropriate words or amounts in the answer blanks.

1. Activities that are thought to cause a cost to be incurred are called activity bases or _____ _____.

2. _____ _____ vary in proportion to changes in the level of activity.

3. The salary of a factory supervisor is an example of a _____ (fixed/variable) cost.

4. _____ _____ remain the same in total dollar amount as the level of activity changes.

5. The rental cost of a piece of office equipment is $2,000 per month plus $1.00 for each machine hour used over 1,500 hours. This is an example of a(n) _____ cost.

6. Mixed costs are sometimes called semivariable or _____ costs.

7. In the high-low method, the difference in total cost divided by the difference in production equals the _____ _____ _____ _____.

8. The _____ _____ is the excess of sales revenue over variable costs.

9. The contribution margin ratio is also called the _____-_____ _____.

10. The _____ _____ ratio measures the effect on operating income of an increase or decrease in sales volume.

11. The unit contribution margin is the dollars from each unit of sales available to cover _____ _____ and provide operating profits.

12. The _____-_____ _____ is the level of operations at which a business's revenues and costs are exactly equal.

13. Increases in property tax rates will cause the break-even point to _____.

14. Decreases in the unit selling price will cause the break-even point to _____.

15. Increases in the unit selling price will cause the break-even point to _____.

16. The vertical axis of a break-even chart depicts _____ and _____.

17. Analyzing the effects of changing selling prices, costs, and volume on the break-even point and profit is called "what if" analysis or _____ _____.

18. The sales volume necessary to break even or to earn a target profit for a business selling two or more products depends upon the _____ _____.

19. If the contribution margin is $200,000 and operating income is $50,000, the operating leverage is _____.

20. An important assumption of cost-volume-profit analysis is that total sales and total costs can be represented by _____ _____.

MULTIPLE CHOICE

Instructions: Circle the best answer for each of the following questions.

1. Which of the following statements describes fixed costs?
   a. costs that remain constant on a per unit basis as the activity base changes
   b. costs that vary in total in direct proportion to changes in the activity base
   c. costs that remain constant on a per unit basis, but vary in total as the activity level changes
   d. costs that remain constant in total dollar amount as the level of activity changes

2. What term is used to describe a cost which has characteristics of both a variable and fixed cost?
   a. variable cost
   b. fixed cost
   c. mixed cost
   d. sunk cost

3. If Berkson Inc.'s costs at 150,000 units of production are $240,000 (the high point of production) and $152,500 at 80,000 units of production (the low point of production), the variable cost per unit using the high-low method of cost estimation is:
   a. 0
   b. $1.25
   c. $1.60
   d. $1.91

4. Which of the following changes would have the effect of increasing the break-even point for a business?

   a. a decrease in fixed costs

   b. a decrease in unit variable cost

   c. a decrease in unit selling price

   d. none of the above

5. Which of the following costs will be classified as a fixed cost in cost-volume-profit analysis?

   a. direct materials

   b. real estate taxes

   c. direct labor

   d. supplies

6. If the contribution margin is $16 and fixed costs are $400,000, what is the break-even point in units?

   a. 25,000

   b. 250,000

   c. 400,000

   d. 6,400,000

7. If sales are $300,000 and sales at the break-even point are $250,000, what is the margin of safety?

   a. 17%

   b. 20%

   c. 83%

   d. 120%

8. If for Jones Inc. the contribution margin is $200,000 and operating income is $40,000, what is the operating leverage?

   a. 240,000

   b. 160,000

   c. 5

   d. .4

9. In cost-volume-profit analysis, variable costs are costs that:

   a. increase per unit with an increase in the activity level

   b. decrease per unit with a decrease in the activity level

   c. remain the same in total at different activity levels

   d. remain the same per unit at different activity levels

10. CM Inc.'s sales are 40,000 units at $12 per unit, variable costs are $8 per unit, and fixed costs are $50,000. What is CM's contribution margin ratio?

    a. 23%

    b. 33%

    c. 50%

    d. 67%

11. B-E Co.'s fixed costs are $120,000, unit selling price is $30, and unit variable cost is $18. What is B-E's break-even point in units?

    a. 4,000

    b. 6,667

    c. 10,000

    d. none of the above

12. Which of the following is a primary assumption of cost-volume-profit analysis?

    a. within the relevant range, the efficiency of operations does not change

    b. costs can be accurately divided into fixed and variable components

    c. sales mix is constant

    d. all of the above

TRUE/FALSE

Instructions: Indicate whether each of the following statements is true or false by placing a check mark in the appropriate column.

	True	False
1. Most operating decisions by management focus on a range of activity, known as the relevant range, within which management plans to operate.................................	____	____
2. Mixed costs, sometimes referred to as semi-variable or semi-fixed costs, are costs that are mostly variable............	____	____
3. The high-low method can be used to estimate the fixed cost and variable cost components of a mixed cost............	____	____
4. Using the high-low method, the fixed costs will differ at the highest and lowest levels of production..............................	____	____
5. The point in the operations of a business at which revenues and expired costs are equal is called the break-even point.	____	____
6. The data required to compute the break-even point are (1) total estimated fixed costs for a future period and (2) the unit contribution margin..	____	____
7. Decreases in the unit selling price will decrease the break-even point.	____	____

8. Decreases in fixed costs will increase the break-even point. .... _____ _____

9. Under variable costing, fixed factory overhead is included in the product cost. .... _____ _____

10. A primary assumption of cost-volume-profit analysis is that the quantity of units in the beginning inventory is equal to the quantity of units in the ending inventory......................... _____ _____

EXERCISE 16-1

Data for the highest and lowest levels of production for Evans Company are as follows:

	Total Costs	Total Units Produced
Highest level	$550,000	50,000 units
Lowest level	$250,000	20,000

Instructions

(1) Determine the differences between total costs and total units produced at the highest and lowest levels of production.

(2) Using the high-low method of cost estimation, estimate the variable cost per unit and the fixed cost for Evans Company.

(3) Based on (2), estimate the total costs for 80,000 units of production.

EXERCISE 16-2

Instructions: Name the following chart and identify the items represented by the letters *a* through *f.*

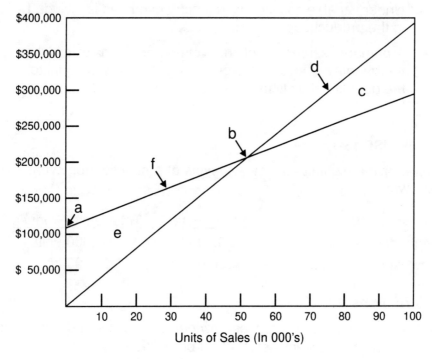

Units of Sales (In 000's)

Chart: _____

(a) _____

(b) _____

(c) _____

(d) _____

(e) _____

(f) _____

EXERCISE 16-3

Instructions: In each of the following cases, use the appropriate formula (margin of safety or operating leverage ratio) to determine the answer.

(1) Sales are $2,000,000.
Break-even sales would be $1,700,000.
The margin of safety as a percentage of sales is ...... _____ %

(2) Sales are $150,000.
Break-even sales would be $100,000.
The margin of safety as a percentage of sales is ...... _____ %

(3) Operating income is $175,000.
The contribution margin is $300,000.
The operating leverage is .... _____

(4) Sales are $700,000.
Variable costs are $300,000.
Operating income is $200,000.
The operating leverage is .... _____

PROBLEM 16-1

Larson Co. produces telephone answering machines. At March 1, Larson estimates fixed costs related to production to be $700,000. The unit selling price,
unit variable cost, and unit contribution margin for Larson Co. are as follows:

Unit selling price $75
Unit variable cost 25
Unit contribution margin $50

Instructions: Perform the following calculations assuming the facts given above,
unless otherwise indicated. (Round to the nearest dollar.)

(1) Calculate the break-even point in units for Larson Co.

(2) Assume Larson Co. is contemplating paying $2,000 more to each of five
factory supervisors. What would the new break-even point be if such a plan
were put into action?

(3) What would the break-even point be if the cost of direct materials increased
by $1.00 per unit?

(4) What would the break-even point be if the selling price increased to $77 per
telephone answering machine?

(5) What is the sales volume necessary to earn a target profit of $300,000?

PROBLEM 16-2

Data related to the expected sales of products A and B for Galla Inc. for the current year, which is typical of recent years, are as follows.

Product	Selling Price per Unit	Variable Cost per Unit	Sales Mix
A	$180	$140	80%
B	$280	$190	20%

The estimated fixed costs for the current year are $400,000.

Instructions:

(1) Determine the estimated sales in units and dollars to reach the break-even point for the current year.

(2) Prove the validity of the answer in (1) by completing the following condensed income statement.

	Product A	Product B	Total
Sales:			
_____ units × $180	_____	_____	_____
_____ units × $280	_____	_____	_____
Total sales	_____	_____	_____
Variable costs:			
_____ units × $140	_____	_____	_____
_____ units × $190	_____	_____	_____
Total variable costs	_____	_____	_____
Contribution margin			_____
Fixed costs			_____
Operating profit			_____

17

Profit Reporting for Management Analysis

QUIZ AND TEST HINTS

The following hints may be helpful to you in preparing for a quiz or a test over the material covered in Chapter 17.

1. Instructors frequently test your understanding of new terms using true/false and multiple-choice questions. As a review of the key terms, do the Matching Exercise on page 775.

2. You will likely see some multiple-choice questions requiring you to calculate the difference between absorption and variable costing income when units manufactured exceed or are less than units sold.

3. Common multiple-choice questions ask you to identify when variable costing income will be less than, equal to, or greater than absorption costing income.

4. You should be able to prepare income statements under both the absorption and variable costing formats.

5. You may be asked to prepare variable costing income statements for products, territories, or salespersons.

FILL IN THE BLANK—Part A

Instructions: Answer the following questions or complete the statements by writing the appropriate words or amounts in the answer blanks.

1. Generally accepted accounting principles require use of the _____ (absorption or variable) concept in determining the cost of goods sold.

2. In the variable costing income statement, deducting variable cost of goods sold from sales yields the _____ _____.

3. The income from operations under absorption costing will be _____ (equal to, greater than, or less than) the income from operations under variable costing when the units sold exceed the units produced.

4. Unlike absorption costing, the variable costing concept treats _____ _____ _____ as a period expense.

5. If the finished goods inventory was 3,000 units after the first month of operations and the fixed factory overhead was $6 per unit, then the income from operations under absorption costing is _____ (amount) _____ (less than or greater than) the income from operations under variable costing.

6. The production volume was 10,000 units, while the sales volume was 12,000 units. The sales price was $40 per unit. The variable cost of goods sold was $28 per unit, and the variable selling and administrative expenses were $7 per unit. The contribution margin shown on the variable costing income statement is _____.

7. For a specific level of management, _____ _____ are costs that can be influenced by management at that level.

8. The _____ _____ refers to the relative distribution of sales among the various products sold.

9–10. Baskins and Taylor are two salespersons that sell Products A and B. The contribution margin of Product A is $40 per unit, while for Product B it is $70 per unit. The total sales volume for both products for each salesperson is as follows:

	Product A	Product B
Baskins	12,000 units	10,000 units
Taylor	8,000	15,000

9. The contribution margin for Product A is _____.

10. The contribution margin for Taylor is _____.

11–12. At the end of the first year of operations, 3,500 units remained in finished goods inventory. The unit manufacturing costs during the year were as follows:

	Unit Costs
Direct materials	$22
Direct labor	20
Variable factory overhead	10
Fixed factory overhead	4

11. The cost of the finished goods inventory reported on the balance sheet under the variable costing income statement is _____.

12. The cost of the finished goods inventory reported on the balance sheet under the absorption costing income statement is _____.

13–16. A business operated at 100% of capacity during its first month of operations with the following results:

Sales (22,500 units)		$1,125,000
Manufacturing costs (25,000 units):		
Direct materials	$300,000	
Direct labor	250,000	
Variable factory overhead	200,000	
Fixed factory overhead	150,000	900,000
Selling and administrative expenses:		
Variable	$146,250	
Fixed	67,500	213,750

13. The amount of the manufacturing margin that would be reported on the variable costing income statement is _____.

14. The amount of income from operations that would be reported on the absorption costing income statement is _____.

15. The amount of contribution margin that would be reported on the variable costing income statement is _____.

16. The amount of income from operations that would be reported on the variable costing income statement is _____.

17. In contribution margin analysis, the factor that is responsible for an increase in the amount of sales due to an increase in price is termed the _____ _____.

18–19. During the current year, 20,000 units were sold at a variable cost of goods sold of $320,000. The sales were planned for 21,500 units at a variable cost of goods sold of $333,250.

18. The amount of difference between the actual and planned variable cost of goods sold due to the quantity factor is _____ _____ (designate amount and direction).

19. The amount of difference between the actual and planned variable cost of goods sold due to the unit cost factor is _____ _____ (designate amount and direction).

20. If the per unit variable selling and administrative expenses were planned to be $2.25 per unit, but were actually $2.00 per unit, then the unit cost factor would result in a(n) _____ (increase or decrease) in contribution margin between planned and actual.

FILL IN THE BLANK—Part B

Instructions: Answer the following questions or complete the statements by writing the appropriate words or amounts in the answer blanks.

1. The term applied to the conventional concept that includes both fixed and variable manufacturing costs as part of the cost of products manufactured is _____ _____.

2. In the variable costing income statement, deducting variable operating expenses from manufacturing margin yields the _____ _____.

3. In the absorption costing income statement, deducting the cost of goods sold from sales yields the _____ _____.

4. In the variable costing income statement, deducting _____ _____ _____ _____ _____ from sales yields the manufacturing margin.

5. The _____ (absorption or variable) costing concept will yield a higher operating income for a period when the number of units manufactured exceeds the units sold.

6. Unlike variable costing, absorption costing treats fixed factory overhead as a(n) _____ cost.

7. The _____ (absorption or variable) costing concept is useful to management in analyzing short-run pricing plans.

8. The _____ (absorption or variable) costing concept is useful to management in analyzing long-run production plans.

9. Direct labor would be _____ (included or excluded) in determining the cost of product under the variable costing concept.

10. Straight-line depreciation on the factory building would be _____ (included or excluded) in determining the cost of product under the variable costing concept.

11–14. A business operated at 100% of capacity during its first month of operations with the following results:

Sales (14,000 units)		$840,000
Manufacturing costs (16,000 units):		
Direct materials	$256,000	
Direct labor	224,000	
Variable factory overhead	128,000	
Fixed factory overhead	80,000	688,000
Selling and administrative expenses:		
Variable	$119,000	
Fixed	56,000	175,000

11. The amount of contribution margin that would be reported on the variable costing income statement is _____.

12. The amount of the manufacturing margin that would be reported on the variable costing income statement is _____.

13. The amount of income from operations that would be reported on the absorption costing income statement is _____.

14. The amount of income from operations that would be reported on the variable costing income statement is _____.

15–16. At the end of the first year of operations, 5,000 units remained in finished goods inventory. The unit manufacturing costs during the year were as follows:

	Unit Costs
Direct materials	$45
Direct labor	26
Variable factory overhead	12
Fixed factory overhead	8

15. The cost of the finished goods inventory reported on the balance sheet under the variable costing income statement is _____.

16. The cost of the finished goods inventory reported on the balance sheet under the absorption costing income statement is _____.

17. In contribution margin analysis, the factor that is responsible for an increase in the amount of sales due to an increase in unit volume is termed the _____ _____.

18–19. During the current year, 12,500 units were sold at a variable cost of goods sold of $187,500. The sales were planned for 12,000 units at a variable cost of goods sold of $192,000.

18. The amount of difference between the actual and planned variable cost of goods sold due to the quantity factor is _____ _____ (designate amount and direction).

19. The amount of difference between the actual and planned variable cost of goods sold due to the unit cost factor is _____ _____ (designate amount and direction).

MULTIPLE CHOICE

Instructions: Circle the best answer for each of the following questions.

1. The manufacturing margin under variable costing is determined by deducting:
   a. equipment depreciation
   b. selling commissions
   c. direct materials
   d. plant manager's salary

2. Which of the following cost elements is included in the cost of goods manufactured under absorption costing but not under variable costing?
   a. direct materials
   b. direct labor
   c. fixed factory overhead
   d. variable factory overhead

3. When units manufactured exceed units sold, the income from operations under absorption costing will be _____ the income from operations under variable costing.
   a. greater than
   b. less than
   c. equal to
   d. either greater than or less than

4. Which of the following would not be deducted in determining the contribution margin under variable costing?
   a. direct labor
   b. sales office depreciation
   c. sales commissions
   d. variable factory overhead

5–6. The contribution margin per unit for Products X and Y are $32 and $65 per unit, respectively. Both products are sold in the Northern and Southern territories in the following volumes:

	Product X	Product Y
Northern	20,000 units	30,000 units
Southern	15,000	11,000

5. The total contribution margin for Product X is:
   a. $640,000
   b. $1,120,000
   c. $1,631,380
   d. $2,275,000

6. The total contribution margin for the Southern territory is:
   a. $832,000
   b. $1,195,000
   c. $1,615,000
   d. $3,785,000

7. Which of the following would not be an appropriate use of variable costing?
   a. pricing products
   b. controlling company-level costs
   c. analyzing market segments
   d. planning production

8. Which of the following is not an example of a market segment?
   a. production department
   b. territory
   c. product
   d. customer

9–10. The planned sales were 16,000 units at a price of $105 per unit. The actual sales were 15,400 units at a price of $112 per unit.

9. The quantity factor is a:
   a. $63,000 decrease
   b. $63,000 increase
   c. $67,200 decrease
   d. $67,200 increase

10. The price factor is a:
   a. $107,800 decrease
   b. $107,800 increase
   c. $112,000 increase
   d. $112,000 decrease

TRUE/FALSE

Instructions: Indicate whether each of the following statements is true or false by placing a check mark in the appropriate column.

		True	False
1.	Absorption costing includes only variable manufacturing costs in the cost of goods manufactured.	_____	_____
2.	Variable selling expenses are deducted in determining the contribution margin.	_____	_____
3.	Fixed factory overhead is deducted in determining the manufacturing margin.	_____	_____
4.	The income from operations determined under variable and absorption costing cannot be equal.	_____	_____
5.	When units manufactured exceed units sold, the income from operations under variable costing is less than under absorption costing.	_____	_____
6.	The variable cost of goods sold would include factory equipment depreciation.	_____	_____
7.	Variable costing should be used for short-term pricing decisions.	_____	_____
8.	Absorption costing should rarely be used for pricing decisions.	_____	_____
9.	Market segment profit analysis should focus on the contribution margin of the segment.	_____	_____
10.	The quantity factor in contribution margin analysis is determined by multiplying the difference between the actual price and the planned price by the actual quantity sold.	_____	_____

EXERCISE 17-1

Power Racquet Inc. manufactures and sells sporting equipment. The company began operations on March 1 and operated at 100% of capacity during the first month. The company produced 45,000 racquets during the month, but sold 42,000 units at $45 per unit. The manufacturing costs and selling and administrative expenses were as follows:

	Total Cost	Number of Units	Unit Cost
Manufacturing costs:			
Variable	$ 810,000	45,000	$18
Fixed	360,000	45,000	8
Total costs	$1,170,000		$26
Selling and administrative expenses:			
Variable ($5 per unit sold)	$ 210,000		
Fixed	160,000		
Total expenses	$ 370,000		
Total costs and expenses	$1,540,000		

Instructions

(1) Prepare an income statement based on the absorption costing concept.

(2) Prepare an income statement based on the variable costing concept.

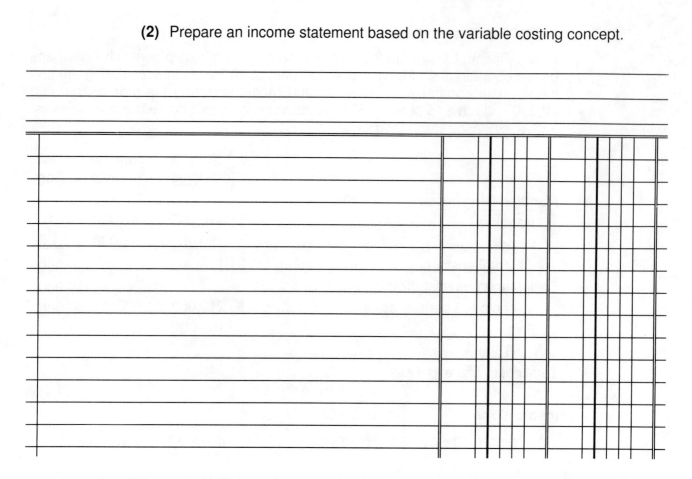

(3) What is the reason for the difference in the amount of income from operations reported in (1) and (2)?

EXERCISE 17-2

On May 31, the end of the first month of operations, Jupiter Company prepared the following income statement based on the absorption costing concept:

Jupiter Company
Income Statement
For the Month Ended May 31, 20--

Sales (46,000 units)		$650,000
Cost of goods sold:		
Cost of goods manufactured	$350,000	
Less inventory, May 31 (4,000 units)	28,000	
Cost of goods sold		322,000
Gross profit		$328,000
Selling and administrative expenses		145,000
Income from operations		$183,000

Instructions: If the fixed manufacturing costs were $140,000 and the variable selling and administrative expenses were $84,000, prepare an income statement according to the variable costing concept.

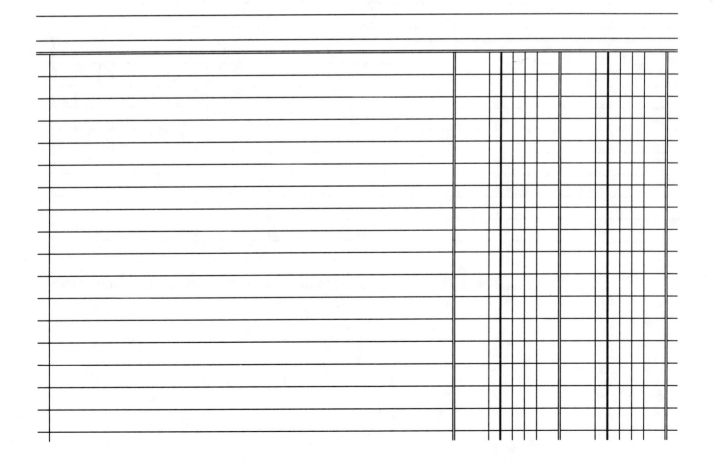

EXERCISE 17-3

Snow Glide Company manufactures and sells two styles of skis—Alpine and Nordic. These skis are sold in two regions—Eastern and Western. Information about the two styles of skis is as follows:

	Alpine	Nordic
Sales price	$350	$400
Variable cost of goods sold per unit	180	280
Manufacturing margin per unit	$170	$120
Variable selling expense per unit	100	100
Contribution margin per unit	$ 70	$ 20
Contribution margin ratio	20%	5%

The sales unit volume for the territories and products for the period is as follows:

	Eastern	Western
Alpine	20,000	40,000
Nordic	30,000	10,000

Instructions

(1) Prepare a contribution margin report by sales territory.

	EASTERN	WESTERN

(2) What advice would you give to the management of Snow Glide Company?

PROBLEM 17-1

During the first month of operations ended June 30, QuickKey Company manufactured 24,000 computer keyboards, of which 22,500 were sold. Operating data for the month are summarized as follows:

Sales		$1,912,500
Manufacturing costs:		
Direct materials	$612,000	
Direct labor	460,800	
Variable manufacturing cost	192,000	
Fixed manufacturing cost	132,000	$1,396,800
Selling and administrative expenses:		
Variable	$270,000	
Fixed	123,750	$ 393,750

Instructions

(1) Prepare an income statement based on the absorption costing concept.

(2) Prepare an income statement based on the variable costing concept.

(3) Explain the reason for the difference in the amount of income from operations reported in (1) and (2).

PROBLEM 17-2

The following data for Ho Company are available for the year ended December 31, 2000:

	Actual	Planned	Difference— Increase or (Decrease)
Sales	$900,000	$814,000	$86,000
Less:			
Variable cost of goods sold	$382,500	$369,600	$12,900
Variable selling and administrative expenses	238,500	246,400	(7,900)
Total	$621,000	$616,000	$ 5,000
Contribution margin	$279,000	$198,000	$81,000
Number of units sold	45,000	44,000	
Per unit:			
Sales price	$20.00	$18.50	
Variable cost of goods sold	$8.50	$8.40	
Variable selling and administrative expenses	$5.30	$5.60	

Instructions: Prepare a contribution margin analysis of the sales and variable costs for Ho Company for the year ended December 31, 2000. Include in your analysis both quantity and unit price/cost factors.

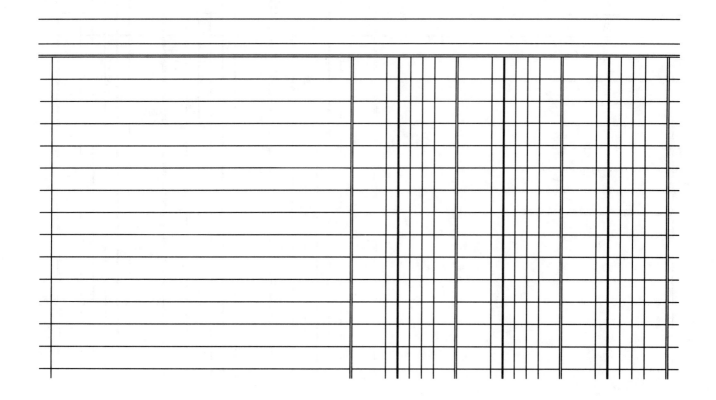

18

Budgeting

QUIZ AND TEST HINTS

The following hints may be helpful to you in preparing for a quiz or a test over the material covered in Chapter 18.

1. Many new terms are introduced in this chapter. You can expect true/false, multiple-choice, or matching questions testing your knowledge of these terms. As a review of the key terms, do the Matching Exercise on page 819.

2. A major emphasis of this chapter is budgeting for manufacturing operations. You should be familiar with all the budgets illustrated in the chapter. The order in which the budgets are normally prepared is the same as that presented in the chapter. For example, the sales budget is normally presented first, followed by the production budget, etc. You may be required to prepare one of these budgets on a test.

3. You can also expect to see some multiple-choice questions that require the computation of the amount of materials to be purchased, units to be produced, cash receipts for a month, etc., as part of the budgeting process.

FILL IN THE BLANK—Part A

Instructions: Answer the following questions or complete the statements by writing the appropriate words or amounts in the answer blanks.

1. The document that charts a course of future action for a business by outlining the plans of the business in financial terms is the _____.

2. Establishing specific goals for future operations is part of the _____ function of management.

3. An organizational unit for which a manager is assigned responsibility over costs, revenues, and assets is called a(n) _____ _____.

4. Comparing actual results to the plan to help prevent unplanned expenditures is part of the _____ function of management.

5. A budget that establishes lower goals than may be possible is said to contain budgetary _____.

6. When individual objectives are opposed to those that are in the best interests of the business, the situation can be described as a(n) _____ _____.

7. The length of time for which the operating budget normally is prepared is a(n) _____ _____.

8. Budgets are usually monitored and summarized by the _____ Department.

9. A(n) _____ budget shows the expected results of a responsibility center for only one activity level.

10. When constructing a flexible budget, the planner must begin by identifying _____ _____ _____.

11. Manufacturing operations require a series of budgets that are linked together in a(n) _____ _____.

12–13. The budget process is started by preparing a sales budget. For each product, the sales budget normally indicates the:

12. _____ ____ _____ _____, and

13. _____ _____ _____ _____.

14. The following data are available from the production budget of O'Connor Inc. for Product X:

Expected units of sales 615,000
Estimated units in beginning inventory 73,500
Total units to be produced 705,500

The desired units in ending inventory are _____.

15. The _____ budget is the starting point for determining the estimated quantities of direct materials to be purchased.

16. The budgets that are used by managers to plan financing, investing, and cash objectives are the _____ _____ _____.

17. The _____ budget presents the expected receipts (inflow) and payments (outflow) of cash for a period of time.

18. The _____ _____ budget summarizes plans for acquiring fixed assets.

19–20. The Townsend Co. production budget for Product X is 300,000 units. Product X is manufactured in two departments. Direct labor in Department 1 is 0.2 hour per unit at an hourly pay rate of $17. Department 2 direct labor requirements for Product X are 0.08 hour per unit at an hourly pay rate of $20.

19. Total hours required for production of Product X are _____.

20. Total direct labor cost is _____.

FILL IN THE BLANK—Part B

Instructions: Answer the following questions or complete the statements by writing the appropriate words or amounts in the answer blanks.

1. Executing actions to meet the goals of the business is the _____ function of management.

2. Giving information to employees about their performance relative to the goals they helped establish is called _____.

3. The budget becomes less effective as a tool for planning or controlling operations if employees view budget goals as unachievable. This occurs when the budget is set too _____.

4. When budgets establish lower goals than may be possible, they are said to be "padded" or to contain _____ _____.

5. The manager of the transportation department was directed to stay within the department budget. To accomplish this goal, the manager stopped shipping to customers for an entire month. This manager's behavior is said to exhibit _____ _____.

6. A variation of fiscal-year budgeting that seeks to maintain a continuous twelve-month projection into the future is called _____ _____.

7. _____-_____ budgeting requires managers to estimate sales, production, and other operating data as though operations are being started for the first time.

8. XYZ Motor Co. establishes its budget at only one level of activity. This type of budget is called a(n) _____ _____.

9. PDQ Construction Co. prepares its budgets based on 8,000, 9,000, and 10,000 units of production. This type of budget is known as a(n) _____ _____.

10. _____ budgeting systems speed up and reduce the cost of preparing budgets.

11. The budget process begins by estimating _____.

12. The production budgets are used to prepare the direct materials purchases, direct labor cost, and _____ _____ _____ budgets.

13. The direct materials purchases, direct labor cost, and factory overhead cost budgets are used to develop the _____ _____ _____ _____ budget.

14. Two major budgets comprising the budgeted balance sheet are the cash budget and the _____ _____ budget.

15. The starting point often used in estimating the quantity of sales for each product in the sales budget is _____ _____ _____.

16. The number of units to be manufactured to meet budgeted sales and inventory needs is set forth in the _____ budget.

17. The _____ _____ _____ budget is prepared based on the production budget and the estimated labor requirements for each unit of product.

18. The _____ _____ _____ allows management to assess the effects of the individual budgets on profits for the year.

19–20. Goldman Inc. uses a flexible budgeting system to plan for its manufacturing operations. The static budget for 9,000 units of production provides for direct labor at $5 per unit and variable electric at $0.60 per unit. Fixed costs are electric power, $1,000, and supervisor salaries of $17,500.

19. Variable costs for 10,000 units of production are _____.

20. Fixed costs for 10,000 units of production are _____.

MULTIPLE CHOICE

Instructions: Circle the best answer for each of the following questions.

1. Which of the following budgets provides the starting point for the preparation of the direct labor cost budget?

    a. direct materials purchases budget

    b. cash budget

    c. production budget

    d. cost of goods sold budget

2. The budget which provides data on the quantities of direct materials purchases necessary to meet production needs is the:

    a. direct materials purchases budget

    b. sales budget

    c. production budget

    d. direct labor cost budget

3. This budget summarizes future plans for the acquisition of plant facilities and equipment.

    a. budgeted balance sheet

    b. production budget

    c. cash budget

    d. capital expenditures budget

4. A series of budgeted amounts for varying levels of activity is called a:

    a. variable budget

    b. continuous budget

    c. flexible budget

    d. zero-based budget

5. Which of the following budgets is used most frequently for administrative functions?

    a. incremental budget

    b. zero-based budget

    c. static budget

    d. flexible budget

6. Assume 80% of sales are collected in the month of sale, with the remainder the following month. Sales for October and November were $640,000 and $860,000, respectively. What are the cash receipts from accounts receivable collections for November?

    a. $684,000

    b. $816,000

    c. $812,000

    d. $860,000

7. A method of budgeting which requires managers to estimate sales, production, and other operating data as though operations were being started for the first time is called:

   a. zero-based budgeting

   b. master budgeting

   c. flexible budgeting

   d. continuous budgeting

8. A method of budgeting which maintains a twelve-month projection into the future is called:

   a. annual budgeting

   b. continuous budgeting

   c. perpetual budgeting

   d. dynamic budgeting

9. An organizational unit with a manager who has authority and responsibility for the unit's performance is called a(n):

   a. economic unit

   b. profit center

   c. budgetary center

   d. responsibility center

10. Assume estimated sales for the coming year is 280,000 units. The estimated inventory at the beginning of the year is 25,000 units, and the desired inventory at the end of the year is 35,000 units. The total production indicated in the production budget is:

   a. 290,000 units

   b. 270,000 units

   c. 305,000 units

   d. 315,000 units

TRUE/FALSE

Instructions: Indicate whether each of the following statements is true or false by placing a check mark in the appropriate column.

	True	**False**
1. A zero-based budget is actually a series of budgets for varying rates of activity.	____	____
2. A budgeting method which provides for maintenance of a twelve-month projection into the future is called continuous budgeting.	____	____
3. Computers are seldom used in the budget process, although computers can reduce the cost of budget preparation.	____	____
4. The number of units of each commodity expected to be manufactured to meet budgeted sales and inventory requirements is set forth in the production budget.	____	____
5. A schedule of collections from sales is useful for developing a cash budget.	____	____
6. The amount of the expenditures for fixed assets such as machinery and equipment usually remains fairly constant from year to year.	____	____
7. Minimum cash balances are maintained to serve as a safety buffer for variations in estimates and for unexpected emergencies.	____	____
8. The budgeted balance sheet brings together the projection of all profit-making phases of operations.	____	____
9. The first budget usually prepared is the cash budget.	____	____
10. The sales budget normally indicates for each product the quantity of estimated sales and the expected unit selling price.	____	____

EXERCISE 18-1

Texier Inc. manufactures two products, C and Q. It is estimated that the May 1 inventory will consist of 8,000 units of C and 21,000 units of Q. Estimated sales for May by sales territory are as follows:

East: Product C — 60,000 units at $15 per unit

          Product Q — 75,000 units at $8 per unit

West: Product C — 80,000 units at $20 per unit

          Product Q — 50,000 units at $10 per unit

An ending inventory of 20% of May sales is desired.

Instructions: Complete the following sales and production budgets for the month of May.

Texier Inc.

Sales Budget

For the Month of May, 20--

PRODUCT AND AREA	UNIT SALES VOLUME	UNIT SELLING PRICE	TOTAL SALES
Product C:			
East area			
West area			
Total			
Product Q:			
East area			
West area			
Total			
Total revenue from sales			

Texier Inc.

Production Budget

For the Month of May, 20--

	UNITS	
	PRODUCT C	PRODUCT Q
Sales		
Plus desired inventory, May 31		
Total		
Less estimated inventory, May 1		
Total production		

EXERCISE 18-2

Instructions: Complete the following factory overhead cost budget for Nathalie Inc. for the month of January. The items listed as variable costs are assumed to vary directly with the units of product. The items listed as fixed costs are assumed to remain constant regardless of units produced.

Nathalie Inc.

Factory Overhead Cost Budget

For the Month of January, 20--

Units of product	30,000	60,000	90,000
Variable cost:			
Indirect factory wages ($.80 per unit)	$ 24 000		
Indirect materials ($.45 per unit)	13 500		
Electric power ($.60 per unit)	18 000		
Total variable cost	$ 55 500		
Fixed cost:			
Supervisory salaries	$ 30 000		
Depreciation of plant and equipment	18 000		
Property taxes	12 000		
Insurance	7 500		
Electric power	4 500		
Total fixed cost	$ 72 000		
Total factory overhead cost	$127 500		

PROBLEM 18-1

The treasurer of Amant Inc. has accumulated the following budget information for the next two months:

	March	April
Sales	$240,000	$200,000
Merchandise costs	150,000	120,000
Operating expenses	60,000	40,000
Capital expenditures	—	125,000

The company expects to sell about 40% of its merchandise for cash. Of sales on account, 80% are expected to be collected in full in the month of the sale and the remainder in the month following the sale. One-third of the merchandise costs are expected to be paid in the month in which they are incurred and the other two-thirds in the following month. Depreciation, insurance, and property taxes represent $20,000 of the probable monthly operating expenses. Insurance is paid in December and a $5,000 installment on property taxes is expected to be paid in March. Of the remainder of the operating expenses, 60% are expected to be paid in the month in which they are incurred and the balance in the following month. Capital expenditures of $125,000 are expected to be paid in April.

Current assets as of March 1 are composed of cash of $24,000 and accounts receivable of $45,000. Current liabilities as of March 1 are composed of accounts payable of $90,000 ($80,000 for merchandise purchases and $10,000 for operating expenses). Management desires to maintain a minimum cash balance of $50,000 at the end of March and April.

Instructions: Prepare a monthly cash budget for March and April.

Amant, Inc.

Cash Budget

For Two Months Ending April 30, 20--

	MARCH	APRIL

PROBLEM 18-2

The Fernandez Furniture Company produces two products, Product A and Product B. The management wishes to budget the sales, production, direct material, and direct labor for the upcoming year. In order to meet this request you have obtained information from various managers throughout the organization. The sales budget was provided by the Sales Department as follows:

Product	Unit Sales Volume	Unit Sales Price	Total Sales
Product A	168,000	$4.20	$ 705,600
Product B	324,000	$8.80	2,851,200
Total			$3,556,800

Information about the inventories for Product A and Product B was obtained by the production manager:

	Product A	Product B
Estimated units in beginning inventory	12,000	24,000
Desired units in ending inventory	8,000	36,000

The materials manager provided information about the materials used in production. There are three different materials used to manufacture Fernandez products: Material X, Material Y, and Material Z. The standard number of pounds required for each unit of Product A and B was determined from the bill of materials:

Standard material pounds per unit	Product A	Product B
Material X	0.6 pounds	1.8 pounds
Material Y		3.4 pounds
Material Z	1.2 pounds	

The purchasing manager provided the standard price per pound for each of the materials:

Material	Price per Pound
Material X	$0.40
Material Y	$0.50
Material Z	$0.60

The materials manager was responsible for the materials inventories and provided the following inventory information:

	Product		
	Material X	Material Y	Material Z
Estimated units in beginning inventory	16,000	5,600	12,400
Desired units in ending inventory	14,500	8,700	9,800

Products A and B are manufactured in two departments, 1 and 2. The industrial engineers provided standard direct labor information from the routing files.

Standard hours per unit	Dept. 1	Dept. 2
Product A	0.20 hours	0.15 hours
Product B	0.05 hours	0.10 hours

The labor rates in each department were provided by the department supervisor for each department.

	Dept. 1	Dept. 2
Labor cost per hour	$14.00	$18.00

Instructions: Construct the following budgets for Fernandez Furniture Company:

(1) Production budget

(2) Direct materials purchases budget

(3) Direct labor cost budget

(1)

Fernandez Furniture Company

Production Budget

	PRODUCT A	PRODUCT B

(2)

Fernandez Furniture Company

Direct Materials Purchases Budget

	MATERIAL X	MATERIAL Y	MATERIAL Z	TOTAL

(3)   *Fernandez Furniture Company*

Direct Labor Cost Budget

	DEPARTMENT 1	DEPARTMENT 2	TOTAL

19

Performance Evaluation Using Variances from Standard Costs

QUIZ AND TEST HINTS

The following hints may be helpful to you in preparing for a quiz or a test over the material covered in Chapter 19.

1. Many new terms are introduced in this chapter. You can expect true/false, multiple-choice, or matching questions testing your knowledge of these terms. As a review of the key terms, do the Matching Exercise on pages 860—861.

2. The major emphasis of this chapter is standard costing. You should be able to compute the six variances illustrated in the chapter. The Illustrative Problem at the end of the chapter is a good study aid for the computation of variances.

3. You also should be able to perform variance analysis based on a flexible budget.

4. Depending upon whether your instructor emphasized standards in the accounts in lecture or through homework, you may be required to prepare journal entries for incorporating standards in the accounts. If your instructor did not cover this topic in class, then do not spend much time studying this section of the chapter.

FILL IN THE BLANK—Part A

Instructions: Answer the following questions or complete the statements by writing the appropriate words or amounts in the answer blanks.

1. Accounting systems that use standards for each element of manufacturing cost entering into the finished product are called _____

   _____ _____.

2. When actual costs are compared with standard costs, only variances are reported for cost control. This reporting philosophy is known as the

   _____ _____ _____.

3. Standards that allow for no idle time, no machine breakdowns, and no materials spoilage are called _____ standards.

4. _____ _____ standards can be attained with reasonable effort and allow for normal production difficulties and mistakes.

5. Standards for direct materials, direct labor, and factory overhead are separated into two components: a price standard and a(n) _____ standard.

6. The _____ department controls the direct materials price per square yard.

7. The difference between the actual cost and the standard cost at the actual volume is called a(n) _____ _____.

8. The sum of the direct materials cost variance, direct labor cost variance, and factory overhead cost variance is the _____ _____ cost variance.

9. The difference between the actual quantity used and the standard quantity at actual production, multiplied by the standard price per unit is the

   _____ _____ _____ _____.

10. If the actual quantity of materials used was 7,000 units at an actual price of $5 per unit and the standard quantity was 6,800 units at a standard price of $5.10 per unit, the materials price variance is _____.

11. The difference between the actual hours worked and the standard hours at actual production, multiplied by the standard rate per hour results in the

    _____ _____ _____ _____.

12. If the actual hours worked are 3,000 at an actual rate per hour of $12 and the standard hours are 3,100 at $11 per hour, the total direct labor cost variance is _____.

13. The _____ variance measures the efficiency of using variable overhead resources.

14. If actual variable factory overhead is $11,400, actual fixed factory overhead is $13,000, and budgeted variable factory overhead for the actual amount produced is $14,400, the controllable variance is _____.

15. The difference between the budgeted fixed overhead at 100% of normal capacity and the standard fixed overhead for actual production achieved is called the _____ _____.

16. The difference between the actual factory overhead and the total overhead applied to production is the _____ _____ _____ _____ variance.

17. The factory overhead cost variance can be verified for each variable factory overhead cost and fixed factory overhead cost element in the _____ _____ _____ _____ _____.

18. A favorable direct materials quantity variance is recorded by crediting _____ _____ _____ _____.

19. At the end of the fiscal year, minor standard cost variances are usually transferred to the _____ _____ _____ _____ account.

20. A way to bring broader perspectives, such as quality of work, to evaluating performance is to supplement financial performance measures with _____ _____ measures.

FILL IN THE BLANK—Part B

Instructions: Answer the following questions or complete the statements by writing the appropriate words or amounts in the answer blanks.

1. A management accounting system that enables management to determine how much a product should cost, how much it does cost, and the causes of any difference is called a(n) _____ _____ _____.

2. Standard setting normally requires the joint efforts of accountants, managers, and _____.

3. Standards that can only be achieved under perfect operating conditions are called _____ _____.

4. Duva Co. assumes normal production difficulties in its standard setting process. These standards are known as _____ _____ standards.

5. The control function of the management process requires actual performance to be compared against the budget. This is known as _____ _____ _____.

6. The actual costs, standard amounts for the actual level of production achieved, and the differences between the two amounts are summarized in the _____ _____ report.

7. When actual cost exceeds budgeted cost at actual volumes, the result is a _____ (favorable/unfavorable) variance.

8. The difference between the actual price per unit and the standard price per unit, multiplied by the actual quantity of materials is the _____ _____ _____ _____.

9. Excessive amounts of direct materials were used by the Hawk Shirt Manufacturing Co. because equipment used in production was not properly maintained and operated. The variance that resulted was a(n) _____ _____ _____ _____.

10. The actual price of direct materials used to manufacture Product B was $0.03 per unit. The standard materials price was established at $0.02. The department responsible for the variance is the _____ _____.

11. If the actual quantity of materials used was 7,000 units at an actual price of $5 per unit and the standard quantity was 6,800 units at a standard price of $5.10 per unit, the total materials cost variance is _____.

12. The difference between the actual rate per hour and the standard rate per hour, multiplied by the actual hours worked is the _____ _____ _____ _____.

13. If the actual hours worked are 3,000 at an actual rate per hour of $12 and the standard hours are 3,100 at $11 per hour, the direct labor time variance is _____.

14. Controlling direct labor cost is normally the responsibility of the _____ _____ _____.

15. The impact of changing production on fixed and variable factory overhead costs can be determined by using a(n) _____ budget.

16. The difference between the actual variable overhead incurred and the budgeted variable overhead for actual production is the variable factory overhead _____ _____.

17. The efficiency of using variable overhead resources is measured by the _____ _____ _____.

18. If budgeted fixed overhead is $12,000, standard fixed overhead for the actual production achieved is $13,000, and actual variable overhead is $13,700, the volume variance is _____.

19. An unfavorable direct materials price variance is recorded by debiting _____ _____ _____ _____.

20. Measuring both financial and _____ performance helps employees consider multiple performance objectives.

MULTIPLE CHOICE

Instructions: Circle the best answer for each of the following questions.

1. Standard costs serve as a device for measuring:

    a. efficiency

    b. nonfinancial performance

    c. volume

    d. quantity

2. Woodson Inc. produced 6,000 light fixtures in May of the current year. Each unit requires 0.75 standard hours. The standard labor rate is $10.00 per hour. Actual direct labor for May was 4,800 hours. What is the direct labor time variance?

    a. $3,000 favorable

    b. $6,000 unfavorable

    c. $3,000 unfavorable

    d. $9,000 favorable

3. The following data relate to direct materials cost for May:

    Standard costs (5,000 lbs. at $2 per lb.) $10,000
    Actual costs (5,100 lbs. at $3 per lb.) 15,300

    What is the direct materials quantity variance?

    a. $200 favorable

    b. $200 unfavorable

    c. $300 favorable

    d. $300 unfavorable

4. Lloyd Company produces music boxes. The standard factory overhead cost at 100% of normal capacity is $100,000 (20,000 hours at $5: $3 variable, $2 fixed). If 700 hours were unused, the fixed factory overhead volume variance would be:

    a. $700 favorable

    b. $1,400 favorable

    c. $2,100 unfavorable

    d. $1,400 unfavorable

5. The Hill Company produced 5,000 units of X. The standard time per unit is .25 hours. The actual hours used to produce 5,000 units of X were 1,350 hours. The standard labor rate is $12.00 per hour. The actual labor cost was $18,900. What is the total direct labor cost variance?

    a. $1,200 unfavorable

    b. $3,900 unfavorable

    c. $1,400 unfavorable

    d. $2,700 unfavorable

6. The cost associated with the difference between the standard quantity and the actual quantity of direct materials used in producing a commodity is called the:

   a. direct materials quantity variance

   b. direct materials price variance

   c. direct materials volume variance

   d. controllable materials variance

7. The cost associated with the difference between the standard hours and the actual hours of direct labor spent producing a commodity is called the:

   a. direct labor quantity variance

   b. direct labor volume variance

   c. direct labor rate variance

   d. direct labor time variance

8. The difference between the budgeted fixed overhead at 100% of normal capacity and the standard fixed overhead for the actual production achieved during the period is called the:

   a. efficiency variance

   b. controllable variance

   c. volume variance

   d. total overhead variance

9. An unfavorable volume variance might be caused by which of the following factors?

   a. an uneven work flow

   b. machine breakdowns

   c. repairs leading to work stoppages

   d. all of the above

10. Which of the following is an example of a nonfinancial performance measure?

    a. number of customer complaints

    b. direct labor time variance

    c. controllable overhead variance

    d. all of the above

TRUE/FALSE

Instructions: Indicate whether each of the following statements is true or false by placing a check mark in the appropriate column.

	True	False
1. Differences between the standard costs of a department or product and the actual costs incurred are termed variances.	____	____
2. If the actual unit price of the materials differs from the standard price, there is a quantity variance.	____	____
3. If the actual direct labor hours spent producing a product differ from the standard hours, there is a direct labor time variance.	____	____
4. The difference between the actual factory overhead and the budgeted factory overhead for the level of production achieved is called the volume variance.	____	____
5. Factory overhead costs are more difficult to manage than are direct labor and materials costs.	____	____
6. At the end of the year, the variances from standard are usually transferred to the work in process account.	____	____
7. A standard level of operation that can be attained with reasonable effort is called an ideal standard.	____	____
8. A useful means of reporting standard factory overhead cost variance data is through a factory overhead cost variance report.	____	____
9. Standards should only be applied in factory settings.	____	____
10. An example of nonfinancial performance measures is the number of customer complaints.	____	____

EXERCISE 19-1

The following data relate to the direct materials and direct labor costs for the production of 10,000 units of product:

<u>Direct Materials</u>
Actual: 77,000 pounds at $1.82 .... $140,140
Standard: 75,000 pounds at $1.80   135,000

<u>Direct Labor</u>
Actual: 42,500 hours at $19.75 .... $839,375
Standard: 42,000 hours at $20.00   840,000

Instructions

(1) Compute the price variance, quantity variance, and total direct materials cost variance.

Price variance:

Quantity variance:

Total direct materials cost variance $ _____

(2) Compute the rate variance, time variance, and total direct labor cost variance.

Rate variance:

Time variance:

Total direct labor cost variance $ _____

EXERCISE 19-2

The following data relate to factory overhead cost for the production of 20,000 units of product:

Actual:	Variable factory overhead	$153,500
	Fixed factory overhead	120,000
Standard:	30,000 hours at $8	240,000

Productive capacity of 100% was 40,000 hours, and the factory overhead cost budgeted at the level of 30,000 standard hours was $270,000.

Instructions: Compute the fixed factory overhead volume variance, variable factory overhead controllable variance, and total factory overhead cost variance. The fixed factory overhead rate was $3 per hour.

Volume variance:

Controllable variance:

Total factory overhead cost variance $ _____

EXERCISE 19-3

During January, Nathalie Inc. manufactured 60,000 units, and the factory overhead costs were: indirect factory wages, $50,500; electric power, $39,500 (included both variable and fixed components); indirect materials, $27,600; supervisory salaries, $30,000; depreciation of plant and equipment, $18,000; property taxes, $12,000; and insurance, $7,500.

Instructions: Prepare a budget performance report for factory overhead for January based on the above data and the factory overhead cost budget shown below.

Nathalie Inc.

Budget Performance Report—Factory Overhead Cost

For Month Ended January 31, 20--

	BUDGET	ACTUAL	UNFAVORABLE	FAVORABLE
Variable cost:				
Indirect factory wages	48000			
Indirect materials	27000			
Electric power	36000			
Total variable cost	111000			
Fixed cost:				
Supervisory salaries	30000			
Depr. of plant and equipment	18000			
Property taxes	12000			
Insurance	7500			
Electric power	4500			
Total fixed cost	72000			
Total factory overhead cost	183000			

EXERCISE 19-4

Each year, a regional IRS office processes thousands of individual tax returns. The standard for processing returns was broken into two types as follows:

Type of Return	Standard Time to Complete Processing
Traditional paper return	45 min.
Return filed electronically	8 min.

By filing their tax returns electronically, individuals reduce the amount of processing time required by the IRS employees.

The regional office employs 30 full time people (40 hrs./wk.) at $16.00 per hour. For the most recent week, the office processed 1,300 traditional returns and 225 electronically filed returns.

Instructions

(1) Compute the amount spent on labor for the week.

(2) Determine the flexible budget in hours for the actual volume for the week.

(3) Compute the time variance.

PROBLEM 19-1

Haley Inc. has established the following standard unit costs:

Materials: 10 lbs. @ $6 per lb.	$ 60.00
Labor: 3 hrs. @ $15 per hr.	45.00
Factory overhead: 3 hrs. @ $3.50 per hr.	10.50
Total standard cost per unit	$115.50

The factory overhead budget includes the following data:

Percent of capacity	85%	100%
Direct labor hours	76,500	90,000
Variable costs	$153,000	$180,000
Fixed costs	135,000	135,000
Total factory overhead cost	$288,000	$315,000
Variable overhead rate per hour		$ 2.00
Fixed overhead rate per hour		1.50
Total overhead rate per hour		$ 3.50

Actual manufacturing costs incurred:

Materials: 250,000 lbs. @ $6.20	$1,550,000
Labor: 77,400 hrs. @ $14.60	1,130,040
Factory overhead (including $135,000 fixed)	295,000
Total actual cost for 25,500 units	$2,975,040
Standard cost of 25,500 units (standard time, 76,500 hrs.) ..	2,945,250
Overall variance to be analyzed (unfavorable)	$ 29,790

Instructions

(1) Determine the price variance and quantity variance for the direct materials cost. Beside the amount of each variance, write the letter F or U to indicate whether the variance is favorable or unfavorable.

<u>Direct Materials Cost Variances</u>

Variance

Price variance:

Actual price .... $_____ per lb.

Standard price .... _____ per lb.

Variance .... $_____ per lb. × actual qty., _____ lbs. $_____

Quantity variance:

Actual quantity .... _____ lbs.

Standard quantity ...... _____ lbs.

Variance .... _____ lbs. × standard price, $_____ _____

Total direct materials cost variance .... $_____

(2) Determine the rate variance and time variance for the direct labor cost. Beside the amount of each variance, write the letter F or U to indicate whether the variance is favorable or unfavorable.

Direct Labor Cost Variances

Variance

Rate variance:

Actual rate .... $ _____ per hr.

Standard rate .... _____ per hr.

Variance .... $ _____ per hr. × actual time, _____ hrs. $ _____

Time variance:

Actual time .... _____ hrs.

Standard time .... _____ hrs.

Variance .... _____ hrs. × standard rate, $ _____ _____

Total direct labor cost variance .... $ _____

(3) Determine the controllable variance and the volume variance for the factory overhead cost. Beside the amount of each variance, write the letter F or U to indicate whether the variance is favorable or unfavorable.

Factory Overhead Cost Variances

Variance

Controllable variance:

Actual variable factory overhead cost incurred ... $ _____

Budgeted variable factory overhead for actual product produced .... _____

Variance .... $ _____

Volume variance:

Budgeted hours at 100% of normal capacity .... _____ hrs.

Standard hours for amount produced .... _____ hrs.

Productive capacity not used .... _____ hrs.

Standard fixed factory overhead cost rate .... $ _____

Variance .... _____

Total factory overhead cost variance .... $ _____

PROBLEM 19-2

The following data were taken from the records of Piazza Company Inc. for January of the current year:

Administrative expenses	$ 42,000
Selling expenses	68,000
Cost of goods sold (at standard)	812,000
Fixed factory overhead volume variance—unfavorable	10,000
Variable factory overhead controllable variance—favorable	4,000
Direct materials quantity variance—unfavorable	1,500
Direct materials price variance—unfavorable	500
Direct labor time variance—favorable	3,000
Direct labor rate variance—unfavorable	1,200
Sales	995,000

Instructions: Prepare an income statement for presentation to management.

Piazza Company, Inc.

Income Statement

For the Month Ended January 31, 20--

20

Performance Evaluation for Decentralized Operations

QUIZ AND TEST HINTS

The following hints may be helpful to you in preparing for a quiz or a test over the material covered in Chapter 20.

1. Many new terms are introduced in this chapter. You can expect true/false, multiple-choice, or matching questions testing your knowledge of these terms. As a review of the key terms, do the Matching Exercise on pages 894–895.

2. The major focus of this chapter is responsibility accounting. Budget performance reports for cost centers have been discussed in earlier chapters, therefore, expect some multiple-choice questions on cost centers. You will probably not have to prepare a budget performance report. You can expect questions requiring you to determine the amount of service department expenses to charge to a profit center, and to calculate income from operations. For investment centers, you should be able to compute rate of return on investment (including the profit margin and investment turnover) and residual income. The Illustrative Problem at the end of the chapter is a good study aid for these computations.

3. This chapter also discusses transfer pricing. Most instructors use multiple-choice questions to cover this topic on tests and quizzes.

FILL IN THE BLANK—Part A

Instructions: Answer the following questions or complete the statements by writing the appropriate words or amounts in the answer blanks.

1. A business operating structure in which all major planning and operating decisions are made by top management can be described as

   _____.

2. Decentralized operating units of a business over which a manager has responsibility are referred to as _____ _____.

3. The process of measuring and reporting operating data by responsibility center is called _____ _____.

4. A responsibility center in which the manager is not required to make decisions concerning sales or the amount of fixed assets invested in the center is called a(n) _____ _____.

5. The principal difference in the responsibility accounting reports provided to higher levels of management is that these reports are _____ (more/less) summarized than for lower levels of management.

6. In a profit center, the manager has the responsibility and authority to make decisions that affect both costs and _____.

7. Costs that can be influenced by the decisions of profit center managers are said to be _____.

8. The costs of services charged to a profit center, based on its use of those services, are called _____ _____

   _____.

9. A measure of the services performed by a service department, which serves as a basis for charging profit centers, is called the _____

   _____.

10. The payroll department processed a total of 50,000 payroll checks and had total expenses of $240,000. If H Division has 10,000 payroll checks for the period, it should be charged _____ for payroll services.

11. If sales are $400,000, cost of goods sold is $235,000, selling expenses are $70,000, and service department charges are $42,000, income from operations is _____.

12. A segment of a business in which the manager has responsibility and authority to make decisions regarding costs, revenues, and invested assets is known as a(n) _____ _____.

13. Income from operations divided by invested assets equals _____

   _____ _____ _____ _____.

14. The ratio of income from operations to sales is called the _____

   _____.

15–17. Income from operations is $70,000, invested assets are $280,000, and sales are $875,000.

   15. The profit margin is _____.

   16. The investment turnover is _____.

   17. The rate of return on investment is _____.

   18. The excess of income from operations over a minimum amount of desired income from operations is termed _____ _____.

   19. Transfer prices can be set as low as the variable cost per unit or as high as the _____ _____.

   20. The _____ _____ approach allows the managers of decentralized units to agree among themselves as to the transfer price.

FILL IN THE BLANK—Part B

Instructions: Answer the following questions or complete the statements by writing the appropriate words or amounts in the answer blanks.

   1. Separating a business into divisions or operating units and delegating responsibility for these units to managers is called _____.

   2. A manager's area of responsibility is called a(n) _____ _____.

   3. Three common types of responsibility centers are cost centers, profit centers, and _____ _____.

   4. Responsibility accounting for cost centers focuses on _____.

   5. Responsibility accounting reports for a supervisor of the mail room would contain _____ (more/less) detailed information than the report issued to the vice-president of administration.

   6. A division over which the manager has the responsibility and the authority to make decisions that affect both costs and revenues is known as a(n) _____ _____.

   7. The manager of the Suit Department of Macy's can influence the amount of salaries paid to departmental personnel. These expenses are said to be _____.

   8. The costs of services provided by the Payroll Department to a profit center within the same company are called _____ _____ _____.

   9. Service department charges are _____ (direct/indirect) expenses to a profit center.

10. The payroll department processed a total of 50,000 payroll checks and had total expenses of $240,000. If J Division has 8,000 payroll checks for the period, it should be charged _____ for payroll services.

11. If sales are $400,000, cost of goods sold is $220,000, selling expenses are $70,000, and service department charges are $42,000, income from operations is _____ .

12. Three measures used to evaluate the performance of investment center managers are income from operations, rate of return on investments, and _____ _____.

13. ROI is calculated by dividing income from operations by _____ _____.

14. The ratio of sales to invested assets is called the _____ _____.

15–17. Income from operations is $70,000, invested assets are $350,000, and sales are $875,000.

15. The profit margin is _____.

16. The investment turnover is _____.

17. The rate of return on investment is _____.

18. Measures of product quality, customer complaints, and warranty expenses are examples of _____ _____ _____.

19. Division A manufactures a radio that is used in the automobile produced in Division B. The charge to Division B for the product is called a(n) _____ _____.

20. Using the _____ _____ approach, the transfer price is the price at which the product or service could be sold to outside buyers.

MULTIPLE CHOICE

Instructions: Circle the best answer for each of the following questions.

1. When the manager has responsibility and authority to make decisions that affect costs, but no responsibility or authority over revenues and assets invested in the department, the department is referred to as:

   a. a cost center

   b. a profit center

   c. an investment center

   d. none of the above

2. If a division organized as a profit center has excess capacity, the most appropriate approach to setting the transfer price is:

   a. market price

   b. negotiated price

   c. cost price

   d. marginal price

3. Which of the following expressions is frequently referred to as the profit margin factor in determining the rate of return on investment?

   a. income from operations divided by invested assets

   b. sales divided by invested assets

   c. income from operations divided by sales

   d. none of the above

4. The manager of which of the following centers has the most authority and responsibility?

   a. cost center

   b. profit center

   c. data center

   d. investment center

5. Division F has sales of $750,000; cost of goods sold of $450,000; operating expenses of $228,000; and invested assets of $300,000. What is the rate of return on investment of Division F?

   a. 9.6%

   b. 10%

   c. 20%

   d. 24%

6. Division F has sales of $750,000; cost of goods sold of $450,000; operating expenses of $228,000; and invested assets of $300,000. What is the investment turnover of Division F?

   a. 1.7

   b. 2.5

   c. 4.2

   d. 10.4

7. The profit margin for Division Q is 15% and the investment turnover is 1.2. What is the rate of return on investment for Division Q?

   a. 12.5%

   b. 15%

   c. 18%

   d. 20%

8. Which of the following is considered an advantage of decentralization?

    a. Decentralized decision making provides excellent training for managers.

    b. Decisions made by different managers all positively affect the overall profitability of the company.

    c. Assets and costs are duplicated across operating divisions.

    d. all of the above

9. Which of the following is an example of a service department?

    a. research and development

    b. purchasing

    c. payroll

    d. all of the above

10. A good example of a nonfinancial performance measure is:

    a. residual income

    b. income from operations

    c. customer retention rate

    d. investment turnover

TRUE/FALSE

Instructions: Indicate whether each of the following statements is true or false by placing a check mark in the appropriate column.

	True	False
1. A primary disadvantage of decentralized operations is that decisions made by one manager may negatively affect the profitability of the entire company.	____	____
2. In an investment center, the manager has responsibility and authority to make decisions that affect not only costs and revenues, but also the assets available to the center.	____	____
3. Responsibility accounting reports for cost centers contain the same amount of detail, regardless of the level of operations to which the report is addressed.	____	____
4. The primary responsibility accounting report for a cost center is the income statement.	____	____
5. Three measures of investment center performance are rate of return on investment, residual income, and income from operations.	____	____
6. Rate of return on investment as a measure of investment center performance reflects not only the revenues and costs of the division, but also the amount of invested assets.	____	____
7. The rate of return on investment is computed by dividing sales by invested assets.	____	____

	True	False

8. If the rate of return on investment is 18% and the invest-
   ment turnover is 3, the profit margin is 9%........................   ____   ____

9. If the divisional profit margin decreases and the investment turnover remains unchanged, the rate of return on
   investment will decrease. ....   ____   ____

10. The market approach to transfer pricing should be used
    when the transferring division has excess capacity. ....   ____   ____

EXERCISE 20-1

Condensed income statements for Divisions M and N of Perlita Inc. and the amount invested in each division are as follows:

		Division M		Division N
Sales		$ 500,000	(c) $	
Cost of goods sold	(a) _____			275,000
Gross profit		$ 220,000		$ 245,000
Operating expenses and service department charges		100,000	(d)	_____
Income from operations	(b) $ _____			$ 110,000
Invested assets		$ 750,000		$ 500,000

Instructions

(1) Insert the amounts of the missing items (a)–(d) in the condensed divisional income statements above.

(2) Determine the rate of return on investment for each division.

(3) On the basis of income from operations, which division is more profitable?

(4) On the basis of rate of return on investment, which division is more profit-able?

EXERCISE 20-2

Based on the data in Exercise 20-1, assume that Perlita Inc. has established a minimum rate of return for invested assets at 12%.

Instructions

(1) Determine the residual income for each division of Perlita.

(2) On the basis of residual income, which division is more profitable?

EXERCISE 20-3

One item is omitted from each of the following computations of the rate of return on investment:

Rate of Return on Investment	=	Profit Margin	×	Investment Turnover
16%		10%		(a) _____
17.5%		(b) _____		1.4
(c) _____		21%		0.9
21.6%		(d) _____		1.2
24%		16%		(e) _____

Instructions: Determine the missing items.

PROBLEM 20-1

The budget for Department F of Plant 7 for the current month ended July 31 is as follows:

Factory wages	$65,000
Materials	39,500
Supervisory salaries	15,000
Power and light	8,900
Depreciation of plant and equipment	7,500
Maintenance	4,300
Insurance and property taxes	2,000

During July, the costs incurred in Department F of Plant 7 were factory wages, $73,600; materials, $37,700; supervisory salaries, $15,000; power and light, $9,600; depreciation of plant and equipment, $7,500; maintenance, $3,900; and insurance and property taxes, $2,000.

Instructions: Prepare a budget performance report for the supervisor of Department F, Plant 7, for the month of July, using the following form:

Budget Performance Report—Supervisor, Department F, Plant 7

For Month Ended July 31, 20--

	BUDGET	ACTUAL	OVER	UNDER

PROBLEM 20-2

Instructions: Using the following information, complete the income statement for Divisions J and K of Firefly Co.

(1)	Division J sales	$280,000
	Division K sales	420,000
(2)	Cost of J sales	122,500
	Cost of K sales	227,500
(3)	Division J operating expenses	48,000
	Division K operating expenses	72,000

The following service department expenses should be charged to the two divisions on the following bases:

(4) Corporate Service Department	Amount	Basis for Charging
Payroll accounting	$60,000	Number of payroll checks
Central purchasing	88,000	Number of requisitions
Brochures	50,000	Number of brochure pages

	Number of Payroll Checks	Number of Requisitions	Number of Brochure Pages
Division J	400	2,200	500
Division K	600	1,800	300
Total	1,000	4,000	800

Firefly Co.

Income Statement—Divisions J and K

For the Year Ended May 31, 20--

	DIVISION J	DIVISION K	TOTAL
Net sales			
Cost of goods sold			
Gross profit			
Operating expenses			
Income from operations before service			
department charges			
Less service department charges:			
Payroll accounting			
Purchasing			
Brochure advertising			
Total service department charges			
Income from operations			

PROBLEM 20-3

TP Co. has two manufacturing divisions, X and Y. Division X currently purchases 10,000 units of materials from an outside supplier at $30 per unit. The same materials are produced by Division Y at a variable cost of $22 per unit. Division Y is operating at full capacity of 40,000 units and can sell all it produces either to outside buyers at $30 or to Division X.

Instructions

(1) Assume that Division Y sells 10,000 units of its product to Division X rather than to outside buyers. If the sale is made at a market price of $30, what will be the effect on:

(a) Division X's income from operations?

_____ increase by $_____

_____ decrease by $_____

_____ no effect

(b) Division Y's income from operations?

_____ increase by $_____

_____ decrease by $_____

_____ no effect

(2) Assume that Division Y sells 40,000 units of product at $30 to outside buyers and still has excess capacity of 10,000 units. If 10,000 units of product are sold to Division X at a negotiated transfer price of $27, what will be the effect on:

(a) Division X's income from operations?

_____ increase by $_____

_____ decrease by $_____

_____ no effect

(b) Division Y's income from operations?

_____ increase by $_____

_____ decrease by $_____

_____ no effect

(3) Assume the same facts as in (2), but use a negotiated transfer price of $20. What will be the effect on:

(a) Division X's income from operations?

_____ increase by $_____

_____ decrease by $_____

_____ no effect

(b) Division Y's income from operations?

_____ increase by $_____

_____ decrease by $_____

_____ no effect

21

Differential Analysis
and Product Pricing

QUIZ AND TEST HINTS

The following hints may be helpful to you in preparing for a quiz or a test over the material covered in Chapter 21.

1. Many new terms are introduced in this chapter. You can expect true/false, multiple-choice, or matching questions testing your knowledge of these terms. As a review of the key terms, do the Matching Exercise on page 933.

2. You can expect short problems testing your ability to perform differential analysis for one or more of the six types of differential analysis illustrations presented in the chapter. Part 5 of the Illustrative Problem at the end of the chapter is a useful study aid for differential analysis of accepting additional business at a special price.

3. You also are likely to see a short problem applying the cost-plus approach to setting product prices. Remember that there are three versions of the cost-plus approach: total cost, product cost, and variable cost. You may find the Key Points on page 930 and the Illustrative Problem at the end of the chapter to be useful study aids.

4. If your instructor emphasized product pricing under production bottlenecks, you might also see a short problem in that area. At least be able to compute the contribution margin per bottleneck hour and describe how this information is used to adjust the product price.

FILL IN THE BLANK—Part A

Instructions: Answer the following questions or complete the statements by writing the appropriate words or amounts in the answer blanks.

1. The amount of increase or decrease in revenue expected from a course of action as compared with an alternative is called _____ _____.

2. The amount of increase or decrease in cost that is expected from a course of action as compared with an alternative is called the _____ _____.

3. In the lease or sell decision regarding a piece of equipment, the book value of the equipment would be considered a(n) _____ _____.

4. In using differential analysis, two additional factors that often need to be considered besides the basic differential revenue and costs are (1) differential revenue from investing the funds generated by the alternatives, and (2) any _____ _____ _____.

5. Product A has a loss from operations of $18,000 and fixed costs of $25,000. All remaining products have income from operations of $75,000 and fixed costs of $30,000. The estimated income from operations if product A is discontinued would be _____.

6. Part Z can be purchased for $30 per unit or manufactured internally for $8 of direct materials, $9 of direct labor, and $15 of factory overhead ($7 of which is fixed). The cost savings from manufacturing part Z internally would be _____.

7. The amount of income that is forgone from an alternative use of cash is called _____ _____.

8. McKeon Gas Co. is deciding whether to sell one of its products at an intermediate stage of development or process it further. The decision will rest on differential revenues and the differential costs of _____ _____.

9. H. Hoch and Co. is considering doing additional business at a special price. If Hoch is operating below full capacity, the differential costs of the additional production are the _____ manufacturing costs.

10. In deciding whether to accept business at a price lower than the normal price, the minimum short-run price should be set high enough to cover all _____ _____.

11–12. The two market methods of setting the normal selling price are:

11. _____-_____.

12. _____-_____.

13. The markup percentage for the total cost concept is determined by dividing desired profit by _____ _____.

14. The markup percentage for the variable cost concept is determined by dividing desired profit plus _____ _____ _____ by total variable costs.

15–17. Product M has total cost per unit of $60, including $20 per unit of selling and administrative costs. Total variable cost is $36 per unit, and desired profit is $6 per unit.

15. The markup percentage based on total cost is _____.

16. The markup percentage based on product cost is _____.

17. The markup percentage based on variable cost is _____.

18. A method of more accurately measuring costs of producing and selling product and focusing on identifying and tracing activities to specific products is known as _____-_____ _____.

19. When the demand for the company's product exceeds its ability to produce the product, the resultant difficulty is referred to as a(n) _____ _____.

20. The manufacturing strategy that focuses on reducing the influence of bottlenecks on a process is the _____ _____ _____.

FILL IN THE BLANK—Part B

Instructions: Answer the following questions or complete the statements by writing the appropriate words or amounts in the answer blanks.

1. A method of decision making that focuses on the effect of alternative courses of action on the relevant revenues and costs is

   _____ _____.

2. Costs that have been incurred in the past that are not relevant to the decision are called _____ _____.

3. The difference between the differential revenue and differential costs is called the _____ _____.

4. The relevant financial factors to be considered in a lease or sell decision are differential costs and _____

   _____.

5. Product B has a loss from operations of $12,000 and fixed costs of $8,000. All remaining products have income from operations of $75,000 and fixed costs of $30,000. The estimated income from operations if product B is discontinued would be _____.

6. Make or buy options often arise when a manufacturer has excess

   _____.

7. A net cash outlay of $225,000 for a new piece of equipment could alternatively be invested to earn 10%. The $22,500 forgone by not investing the funds is called a(n) _____ _____.

8. Product K is produced for $4 per gallon and can be sold without additional processing for $5 per gallon. Product K can be processed further into product G at a cost of $2 per gallon ($.80 fixed). Product G can be sold for $6.50 per gallon. The differential income per gallon from processing product K into product G is _____.

9. The law that prohibits price discrimination within the United States, unless differences in prices can be justified by different costs of serving different customers, is the _____-_____

   _____.

10–12. The three cost concepts used in applying the cost-plus approach to setting normal product prices are:

   10. _____ _____.

   11. _____ _____.

   12. _____ _____.

13. Under the _____ _____ concept, all costs of manufacturing a product plus the selling and administrative expenses are included in the cost amount to which the markup is added.

14. Contractors who sell products to government agencies often use the _____ _____ concept of applying the cost-plus approach to product pricing.

15. The markup percentage for the product cost concept is determined by dividing desired profit plus total selling and administrative expenses by

_____ _____ _____.

16–18. Product N has total cost per unit of $40, including $15 per unit of selling and administrative costs. Total variable cost is $30 per unit, and desired profit is $5 per unit.

16. The markup percentage based on total cost is _____.

17. The markup percentage based on product cost is _____.

18. The markup percentage based on variable cost is _____.

19. A cost concept, pioneered by the Japanese, that assumes that the selling price is set by the marketplace is the _____

_____ _____.

20. The term used to describe a situation when the demand for a company's product exceeds the ability of the company to produce it is

_____ _____.

MULTIPLE CHOICE

Instructions: Circle the best answer for each of the following questions.

1. The area of accounting concerned with the effect of alternative courses of action on revenues and costs is called:

   a. gross profit analysis

   b. capital investment analysis

   c. differential analysis

   d. cost-volume-profit analysis

2. A business received an offer from an exporter for 10,000 units of product at $18 per unit. The acceptance of the offer will not affect normal production or the domestic sales price. The following data are available:

   Domestic sales price $25
   Unit manufacturing costs:
       Variable 16
       Fixed 4

   What is the amount of gain or loss from acceptance of the offer?

   a. $20,000 gain

   b. $20,000 loss

   c. $70,000 gain

   d. $70,000 loss

3. The amount of income that is forgone from the best available alternative to the proposed use of cash or its equivalent is called:

   a. sunk cost

   b. opportunity cost

   c. differential cost

   d. opportunity revenue

4. For which cost concept used in applying the cost-plus approach to product pricing are total selling and general expenses and desired profit allowed for in the determination of markup?

   a. total cost

   b. product cost

   c. variable cost

   d. none of the above

5. A business produces Product A in batches of 5,000 gallons, which can be sold for $3 per gallon. The business has been offered $5 per finished gallon to process two batches of Product A further into Product B. Product B will require additional processing costs of $7,800 per batch, and 10% of the gallons of Product A will evaporate during processing. What is the amount of gain or loss from further processing of Product A?

   a. $12,200 gain

   b. $7,200 gain

   c. $4,400 gain

   d. $600 loss

6. Which of the following cost concepts is not used in applying the cost-plus approach to setting the selling price?

   a. product cost

   b. total cost

   c. variable cost

   d. fixed cost

7. Which of the following concepts accepts product price as given by the marketplace?

   a. total cost plus markup concept

   b. variable cost plus markup concept

   c. target cost concept

   d. product cost plus markup concept

8. The Majestic Company's casting operation is a production bottleneck. Majestic produces three products with the following per unit characteristics.

	Product A	Product B	Product C
Sales price	$100	$120	$200
Variable cost per unit	40	50	120
Contribution margin per unit	60	70	80
Fixed cost per unit	10	30	50
Net profit per unit	50	40	30
Casting time	3.5 hrs.	3 hrs.	4 hrs.

   Which product is the most profitable to the company?

   a. Product A

   b. Product B

   c. Product C

   d. Products A and C

9. Which of the following is a market method of setting the selling price?

   a. competition-based

   b. total cost-based

   c. variable cost-based

   d. product cost-based

10. Management is considering replacing its blending equipment. The annual costs of operating the old equipment are $250,000. The annual costs of operating the new equipment are expected to be $220,000. The old equipment has a book value of $35,000 and can be sold for $25,000. The cost of the new equipment would be $260,000. Which of these amounts should be considered a sunk cost in deciding whether to replace the old equipment?
    a. $250,000
    b. $220,000
    c. $35,000
    d. $25,000

TRUE/FALSE

Instructions: Indicate whether each of the following statements is true or false by placing a check mark in the appropriate column.

	True	False
1. In deciding whether to replace fixed assets, the book values of the fixed assets being replaced are sunk costs and are irrelevant.		
2. The amount of increase or decrease in cost that is expected from a particular course of action as compared with an alternative is called opportunity cost.		
3. In deciding whether to accept business at a special price, a company which is operating below full capacity will decrease its operating income if the special price does not exceed all costs.		
4. Discontinuance of an unprofitable segment of business will usually eliminate all of the related fixed costs.		
5. The amount of income that would result from the best available alternative to the proposed use of cash or its equivalent is called differential cost.		
6. Using the total cost concept of applying the cost-plus approach to product pricing, all costs of manufacturing the product plus the selling and administrative expenses are included in the cost amount to which the markup is added.		
7. In differential analysis, two additional factors to be considered in making a lease or sell decision are (1) differential revenue from investing funds generated by alternatives and (2) any income tax differential.		

True   False

8. Using the cost-plus approach to product pricing, managers determine product prices by adding a markup to a cost amount..   _____   _____

9. Contractors who sell to government agencies often use the total cost approach to product pricing. ....   _____   _____

10. The best way to measure product profitability in a production bottleneck environment is with contribution margin per unit. ....   _____   _____

EXERCISE 21-1

Walden Transportation Inc. has a truck that it no longer needs. The truck can be sold for $18,000 or it can be leased for a period of 5 years at $4,000 per year. At the end of the lease, the truck is expected to be sold for a negligible amount. The truck cost $50,000 four years ago, and $35,000 depreciation has been taken on it to date. To be sold for $18,000, the truck must first be repainted at a cost of $900. If the truck is to be leased for the 5-year period, Walden must provide the licenses, which cost $220 per year. The lessee must provide insurance at an annual cost of $200, tires at an estimated annual cost of $600, and repairs that are expected to amount to $2,000 during the 5-year period.

Instructions: Complete the following form to determine which alternative is more advantageous to Walden Transportation Inc. and to determine the amount of that advantage. (Ignore the fact that if the truck is leased, not all of the revenue is received at once.)

Walden Transportation Inc.
Proposal to Lease or Sell Truck

Differential revenue from alternatives:		
Revenue from lease	$_____	
Revenue from sale	_____	
Differential revenue from lease		$_____
Differential cost of alternatives:		
License expenses during lease	$_____	
Repainting expense on sale	_____	
Differential cost of leasing		_____
Net differential income (loss) from lease alternative ...		$_____

EXERCISE 21-2

Tran Inc. has been purchasing metal blades for $14 a set for use in producing food processors. The cost of manufacturing the blades is estimated at $6.75 for direct materials, $5.10 for direct labor, and $1.80 for factory overhead ($1.00 fixed and $.80 variable). Because there is unused capacity available, there would be no increase in the total amount of fixed factory overhead costs if Tran manufactures the blades.

Instructions: Complete the following form to determine whether Tran Inc. should make or buy the blades.

Tran Inc.
Proposal to Manufacture Metal Blades

Purchase price of blades		$_____
Differential cost to manufacture blades:		
Direct materials	$_____	
Direct labor	_____	
Variable factory overhead	_____	_____
Cost savings (increase) from manufacturing blades ...		$_____

EXERCISE 21-3

English Chairs Inc. produces a line of rocking chairs in one section of the plant, and stuffed chairs and recliner chairs in other sections. The controller has supplied the following condensed income statement for the year just ended:

English Chairs Inc.
Condensed Income Statement
For Year Ended December 31, 20--

	Stuffed Chairs	Recliner Chairs	Rocking Chairs	Total
Sales	$500,000	$250,000	$350,000	$1,100,000
Cost of goods sold:				
Variable costs	$250,000	$110,000	$180,000	$ 540,000
Fixed costs	50,000	30,000	90,000	170,000
Total cost of goods sold	$300,000	$140,000	$270,000	$ 710,000
Gross profit	$200,000	$110,000	$ 80,000	$ 390,000
Operating expenses:				
Variable expenses	$100,000	$ 60,000	$75,000	$ 235,000
Fixed expenses	60,000	25,000	43,000	128,000
Total operating expenses	$160,000	$ 85,000	$118,000	$ 363,000
Income (loss) from operations	$ 40,000	$ 25,000	$ (38,000)	$ 27,000

Instructions: Complete the following form and determine whether the rocking chairs section should be continued.

English Chairs Inc.
Proposal to Discontinue Rocking Chairs
December 31, 20--

Differential revenue from sales of rocking chairs:

    Revenue from sales .... $ _____

Differential cost of sales of rocking chairs:

    Variable cost of goods sold .... $ _____

    Variable operating expenses .... _____ _____

Differential income (loss) from sales of rocking chairs .... $ _____

The rocking chairs section probably _____ be continued.

EXERCISE 21-4

Golub Inc. has a machine which cost $250,000 five years ago and has $155,000 accumulated depreciation to date. The company can sell the machine for $83,000 and replace it with a larger one costing $370,000. The variable annual operating cost of the present machine amounts to $65.000. The variable annual operating cost of the new machine is estimated to be $30,000. It is estimated that either machine could be used for seven years from this date, December 31, 20--, and that at the end of the seven-year period neither would have a significant residual value.

Instructions: Complete the following schedule and determine the advisability of replacing the present machine.

Golub Inc.
Proposal to Replace Machine
December 31, 20--

Annual variable costs—present machine	$ _____	
Annual variable costs—new machine	_____	
Annual differential decrease (increase) in variable costs	$ _____	
Number of years applicable	_____	
Total differential decrease (increase) in variable costs	$ _____	
Proceeds from sale of present machine	_____	$ _____
Cost of new machine		_____
Net differential decrease (increase) in cost, seven-year total		$ _____
Annual net differential decrease (increase) in cost—new machine		$ _____

PROBLEM 21-1

Smith Company recently began production of a new product, G, which required the investment of $500,000 in assets. The costs and expenses of producing and selling 50,000 units of Product G are as follows:

Variable costs:

Direct materials	$1.20 per unit
Direct labor	2.40
Factory overhead	.40
Selling and administrative expenses	1.00
Total	$5.00 per unit

Fixed costs:

Factory overhead	$35,000
Selling and administrative expenses	15,000

Smith Company is currently establishing a selling price for Product G. The president of Smith Company has decided to use the cost-plus approach to product pricing and has indicated that Product G must earn a 12% rate of return on invested assets.

Instructions

(1) Determine the amount of desired profit from the production and sale of Product G.

(2) Assuming that the total cost concept is used, determine (a) the cost amount per unit, (b) the markup percentage, and (c) the selling price of Product G.

   (a)

   (b)

   (c)

PROBLEM 21-2

Based upon the data in Problem 21-1, assume that Smith Company uses the product cost concept of product pricing.

Instructions: Determine (1) the cost amount per unit, (2) the markup percentage, and (3) the selling price of Product G. (Round to the nearest cent.)

(1)

(2)

(3)

PROBLEM 21-3

Based upon the data in Problem 21-1, assume that Smith Company uses the variable cost concept of product pricing.

Instructions: Determine (1) the cost amount per unit, (2) the markup percentage, and (3) the selling price of Product G.

(1)

(2)

(3)

PROBLEM 21-4

The Zelda Company produces three products, Products D, E, and F. All three products require heat treatment in a furnace operation. The furnace operation is a production bottleneck. The annual cost of the furnace operation is $180,000. Information about the three products is as follows:

	Product D	Product E	Product F
Sales price per unit	$750	$600	$400
Variable cost per unit	300	350	200
Contribution margin per unit	$450	$250	$200
Fixed cost per unit	200	200	150
Profit per unit	$250	$ 50	$ 50
Furnace hours per unit	15	10	8

Instructions: Determine the price for Products E and F that would generate the same profitability as Product D.

22

Capital Investment Analysis

QUIZ AND TEST HINTS

The following hints may be helpful to you in preparing for a quiz or a test over the material covered in Chapter 22.

1. Many new terms are introduced in this chapter. You can expect true/false, multiple-choice, or matching questions testing your knowledge of these terms. As a review of the key terms, do the Matching Exercise on page 966.

2. You can expect some problems requiring you to perform capital investment analysis using each of the four methods illustrated in the chapter. Often, instructors will use multiple-choice questions to test your knowledge of the average rate of return method, cash payback method, and present value index. Short problems will be used to test your knowledge of the net present value and internal rate of return methods. The chapter illustrations and the Illustrative Problem at the end of the chapter are good study aids.

3. The remaining chapter topics are tested most often using true/false or multiple-choice questions. The Key Points at the end of the chapter are a good, concise review for many of these items.

FILL IN THE BLANK—Part A

Instructions: Answer the following questions or complete the statements by writing the appropriate words or amounts in the answer blanks.

1. The process by which management plans, evaluates, and controls invest-ments in fixed assets is called _____ _____ _____.

2. Two methods for evaluating capital investment proposals using present values are the net present value method and the _____ _____ _____ _____ method.

3. The methods that ignore present value are often useful in evaluating capi-tal investment proposals that have relatively _____ useful lives.

4. Mist Company is considering whether or not to buy a new machine costing $400,000. The machine has a useful life of 8 years, with a residual value of $28,000, and is expected to produce average yearly revenues of $53,500. The average rate of return on this machine is _____.

5. One advantage of the _____ _____ _____ _____ method is that it emphasizes accounting income, which is often used by investors and creditors in evaluating management performance.

6. The _____ _____ period is the amount of time that will pass between the date of the investment and the complete recovery of the funds invested.

7. A new machine will cost $15,000 per year to operate and is expected to generate $65,000 in revenues. The machine is expected to last for 10 years and will cost $300,000. The cash payback period on this investment is _____.

8. Managers who are primarily concerned with liquidity will prefer to use the _____ _____ method of evaluating capital investments.

9. A series of equal net cash flows at fixed intervals is called a(n) _____.

10. The _____ _____ _____ method analyzes capital investment proposals by comparing the initial cash investment with the present value of the net cash flows.

11. A project has estimated annual net cash flows of $50,000 for 5 years and is estimated to cost $180,000. Assuming a minimum rate of return of 10%, the net present value of this project is _____.

12. A present value _____ is calculated by dividing the total present value of the net cash flow by the amount to be invested.

13. An advantage of the _____ _____ _____ method is that it considers the time value of money.

14. The present value factor for an annuity is calculated by dividing the total amount to be invested by the equal _____ _____ _____ _____ created by the investment.

15. A company is using the internal rate of return method to appraise a capital investment decision. Several proposals have been ranked according to their internal rate of return. The company should choose the proposal with the _____ (highest/lowest) rate of return.

16. Factors that complicate capital investment analysis include federal income tax, unequal lives of alternative proposals, leasing, _____, changes in price levels, and qualitative factors.

17. To evaluate capital investment alternatives with different useful lives, net present values should be adjusted so that each alternative ends at the _____ time.

18. Investments designed to affect a company's long-term ability to generate profits are called _____ investments.

19. Product quality, manufacturing flexibility, employee morale, manufacturing productivity, and manufacturing control are _____ considerations affecting capital investment analysis.

20. In capital rationing, alternative proposals are initially screened by establishing _____ standards for the cash payback and the average rate of return.

FILL IN THE BLANK—Part B

Instructions: Answer the following questions or complete the statements by writing the appropriate words or amounts in the answer blanks.

1. Methods of evaluating capital investment proposals can be grouped into two categories based on whether or not they involve _____ _____.

2. Two methods for evaluating capital investment proposals that do not use present values are the average rate of return method and the _____ _____ method.

3. The _____ _____ of money concept recognizes that an amount of cash invested today will earn income and therefore has value over time.

4. The _____ _____ _____ _____ is a measure of the average income as a percent of the average investment in fixed assets.

5. The average rate of return for a project that is estimated to yield total income of $270,000 over three years, cost $680,000, and has a $40,000 residual value is _____.

6. The excess of cash flowing in (from revenues) over the cash flowing out (for expenses) is called the _____ _____ _____.

7. When annual net cash flows are not equal, the _____ _____ _____ is determined by adding the annual net cash flows until the cumulative sum equals the amount of the proposed investment.

8. Present value methods for evaluating capital investment proposals consider both the amounts and the _____ of net cash flows.

9. The sum of the present values of a series of equal net cash flows is known as the _____ _____ _____ _____ _____.

10. If the _____ _____ _____ of the cash flows expected from a proposed investment equals or exceeds the amount of the initial investment, the proposal is desirable.

11. Shine Company is using the net present value method to evaluate an investment. The investment will cost $60,000, is expected to last for 3 years, and will generate annual returns of $30,000. The desired rate of return is 12%. The net present value of this investment is _____.

12. Project X costs $50,000 and has a total present value of $72,000. The present value index is _____.

13. The _____ _____ _____ _____ method uses present value concepts to compute the rate of return from the net cash flows expected from capital investment proposals.

14. You are using the internal rate of return method to evaluate an investment alternative. You can buy new equipment costing $26,500. The equipment has a useful life of 4 years and is expected to produce annual cash flows of $10,000. Assuming a 10% rate of return, the net present value of this investment is _____.

15. A new fabricating machine will cost $79,600 and will generate equal annual revenues of $16,000. The present value factor of this machine is

_____.

16. The primary advantage of the _____ _____ _____ _____ method is that the present values of the net cash flows over the entire useful life of the proposal are considered.

17. _____ allows a business to use fixed assets without spending large amounts of cash to purchase them and may be evaluated using capital investment analysis techniques.

18. A period of increasing prices, sometimes called a period of _____, can significantly affect capital investment analysis.

19. Capital _____ is the process by which management allocates funds among competing capital investment proposals.

20. Qualitative considerations in capital investment analysis are most appropriate for _____ _____.

MULTIPLE CHOICE

Instructions: Circle the best answer for each of the following questions.

1. Which of the following methods of evaluating capital investment proposals ignores present value concepts?
   a. average rate of return method
   b. discounted cash flow method
   c. discounted internal rate of return method
   d. none of the above

2. The method of evaluating capital investment proposals which determines the total present value of cash flows expected from investment proposals and compares these values with the amounts to be invested is:
   a. average rate of return method
   b. cash payback method
   c. discounted internal rate of return method
   d. discounted cash flow method

3. The method of evaluating capital investment proposals which uses present value concepts to compute the rate of return from the net cash flows expected from the proposals is:
   a. average rate of return method
   b. cash payback method
   c. internal rate of return method
   d. discounted cash flow method

4. Jones Inc. is considering the purchase of a machine that costs $360,000. The machine is expected to have a useful life of 10 years, with no salvage value, and is expected to yield an annual net cash flow of $120,000 and an annual operating income of $60,000. What is the estimated cash payback period for the machine?
   a. 2 years
   b. 3 years
   c. 5 years
   d. 6 years

5. Management is considering an $800,000 investment in a project with a 6-year life and no residual value. If the total income from the project is expected to be $600,000 and recognition is given to the effect of straight-line depreciation on the investment, the average rate of return is:
   a. 12.5%
   b. 25%
   c. 32%
   d. 44%

6. Which of the following is a qualitative consideration that may impact upon capital investment analysis?

   a. manufacturing flexibility

   b. expected net cash inflows

   c. amounts of cash to be invested

   d. timing of cash inflows

7. Genko Company has purchased a machine for $145,000. The machine is expected to generate a positive annual net cash flow of $50,000 for four consecutive years. What is the present value index, assuming a minimum rate of return of 10%?

   a. 0.942

   b. 0.915

   c. 1.093

   d. 1.379

8. The net present value method is also called the:

   a. internal rate of return method

   b. time-adjusted rate of return method

   c. average rate of discounted return method

   d. discounted cash flow method

9. A disadvantage of the cash payback method is that it:

   a. focuses on measures that are not important to bankers and other creditors

   b. emphasizes accounting income

   c. does not use present value concepts in valuing cash flows occurring in different periods

   d. cannot be used when annual net cash flows are not equal

10. Which of the following factors may have an impact on a capital investment decision?

    a. federal income taxes

    b. unequal lives of proposed investments

    c. changes in price levels

    d. all of the above

TRUE/FALSE

Instructions: Indicate whether each of the following statements is true or false by placing a check mark in the appropriate column.

	True	False

1. The two common present value methods used in evaluating capital investment proposals are (1) the net present value method and (2) the internal rate of return method. ..... ____   ____

2. Two methods of evaluating capital investment proposals that ignore present value are (1) the average rate of return method and (2) the cash payback period method. .... ____   ____

3. The expected time that will pass between the date of capital investment and the complete recovery of cash (or equivalent) of the amount invested is called the present value period. .... ____   ____

4. The methods of evaluating capital investment proposals that ignore present value are especially useful in evaluating capital investments that have relatively long useful lives. .... ____   ____

5. The net present value method, sometimes called the internal rate of return or time-adjusted rate of return method, uses present value concepts to compute the rate of return from the net cash flows expected from the capital investment proposals. .... ____   ____

6. The present value index is computed by dividing the amount to be invested by the total present value of the net cash flow. .... ____   ____

7. The present value factor for an annuity of $1 is computed by dividing the amount to be invested by the annual net cash flow. .... ____   ____

8. Proposals that are funded in the capital rationing process are included in the capital expenditures budget to aid the planning and financing of operations. .... ____   ____

9. One advantage of the average rate of return method is that it includes the amount of income earned over the entire life of the proposal. .... ____   ____

10. One disadvantage of the cash payback method is that it includes cash flows occurring after the payback period. ..... ____   ____

EXERCISE 22-1

Daily Inc. is considering the acquisition of a newly developed machine at a cost of $620,000. This machine is expected to have a useful life of 5 years and no residual value. Use of the new machine is expected to yield total income of $240,000 during the 5 years of its useful life and to provide an average annual net cash flow of $200,000. The minimum rate of return desired by Daily is 12%. The maximum cash payback period desired by Daily is 3 years.

Instructions: Using the information given, make the analyses indicated and write your answers in the spaces provided.

(1) What average rate of return (based on the average investment) can Daily expect to achieve during the useful life of this machine? .... _____ %

(2) What is the expected cash payback period for this proposed expenditure? .... _____ years

(3) Based on the analysis of average rate of return, should the management of Daily acquire the new machine? ...   yes_____ no_____

(4) Based on the expected cash payback period, should management acquire the new machine? ....   yes_____ no_____

EXERCISE 22-2

Crusty Corp. is evaluating two capital investment proposals, each requiring an investment of $250,000 and each with a six-year life and expected total net cash flows of $360,000.

Proposal 1 is expected to provide equal annual net cash flows of $60,000. Proposal 2 is expected to have the following unequal net cash flows:

Year 1	$100,000	Year 4	$45,000
Year 2	80,000	Year 5	45,000
Year 3	70,000	Year 6	20,000

Instructions: Determine the cash payback period for each proposal.

Proposal 1:

Proposal 2:

EXERCISE 22-3

Assume that Crusty Corp. is re-evaluating the two capital investment proposals described in Exercise 22-2, taking into consideration present value concepts.

Instructions: Determine the net present value for each proposal using a rate of 10%.

Proposal 1:

Proposal 2:

EXERCISE 22-4

The management of Argo Inc. has decided to use the internal rate of return method to analyze a capital investment proposal that involves an investment of $358,900 and annual net cash flows of $120,000 for each of the 5 years of useful life.

Instructions

(1) Determine the present value factor for an annuity of $1 which can be used in determining the internal rate of return.

(2) Using the factor determined in (1) and the present value of an annuity of $1 table appearing in Chapter 22, determine the internal rate of return for the proposal.

PROBLEM 22-1

Instructions

(1) Complete the following table using the net present value method to evaluate capital investment in new equipment.

Year	Present Value of 1 at 12%	Net Cash Flow	Present Value of Net Cash Flow
1	0.893	$ 80,000	$ _____
2	0.797	60,000	_____
3	0.712	60,000	_____
4	0.636	60,000	_____
5	0.567	60,000	_____
Total		$320,000	$ _____
Amount to be invested in equipment			180,000
Excess of present value over amount to be invested ..			$ _____

(2) Compute the present value index for the new equipment. (Round to two decimal places.)

(3) Based on the net present value method, should management acquire the new machine? .... yes_____ no_____

PROBLEM 22-2

Preston Co. is evaluating two projects which have different useful lives but which have an equal investment requirement of $180,000. The estimated net cash flows from each project are as follows:

Year	Project 1	Project 2
1	$55,000	$55,000
2	50,000	55,000
3	45,000	55,000
4	40,000	55,000
5	40,000	55,000
6	30,000	
7	15,000	

Preston Co. has selected a rate of 10% for purposes of net present value analysis. Preston also estimates that there will be no residual value at the end of each project's useful life, but at the end of the fifth year, Project 1's residual value would be $60,000.

Instructions

(1) For each project, compute the net present value.

(2) For each project, compute the net present value, assuming that Project 1 is adjusted to a five-year life for purposes of analysis.

(3) Determine which of the two projects is more attractive based upon your findings in (2) above.

23

Cost Allocation and Activity-Based Costing

QUIZ AND TEST HINTS

The following hints may be helpful to you in preparing for a quiz or a test over the material covered in Chapter 23.

1. This chapter introduces new terms related to cost allocation and activity-based costing. Instructors normally test this material using true/false and multiple-choice questions. As a review of the key terms, do the Matching Exercise on page 999.

2. The chapter focuses on demonstrating three different methods of allocating factory overhead: the plantwide rate method, the multiple production department rate method, and the activity-based costing method. Expect problems requiring you to determine product costs under these methods. You may be asked to compare and explain the difference in results obtained from using different methods with the same underlying information. The Illustrative Problem on pages 997–999 in the text is a good study aid.

3. Be prepared to explain the conditions that favor the use of the single plantwide rate method, the multiple production department rate method, and the activity-based costing method.

4. The activity-based costing method is illustrated in the chapter for factory costs, selling and administrative expenses, and service companies. Expect a problem using activity-based costing in one or more of these scenarios.

5. Be prepared to explain the difference between using activity-based costing and relative sales-volume allocation for selling and administrative expenses.

6. Expect some multiple-choice questions using the simpler plantwide rate allocation and the more complex activity-based costing approach.

FILL IN THE BLANK—Part A

Instructions: Answer the following questions or complete the statements by writing the appropriate words or amounts in the answer blanks.

1. Determining the cost of a product is called _____ _____.

2. The single plantwide factory overhead rate is determined by dividing _____ _____ _____ _____ _____ by _____ _____ _____ _____ _____.

3. The factory overhead allocated to a product with 24 machine hours, using a single plantwide factory overhead rate of $12 per machine hour, is _____.

4. Under the multiple production department factory overhead rate method there is a factory overhead rate for each _____ _____.

5. An Assembly Department has budgeted factory overhead of $420,000 and 7,000 estimated direct labor hours; thus, the Assembly Department factory overhead rate is _____.

6. If the Packing Department has a departmental factory overhead rate of $32 per direct labor hour, then a product requiring 15 hours in the Packing Department will be allocated _____ of Packing Department factory overhead cost.

7. When some products are allocated too much cost, while others are allocated too little cost, the cost allocation method is said to lead to product cost _____.

8. The total factory overhead cost allocated by the single plantwide rate method is _____ (less than, equal to, or greater than) the cost allocated by the multiple production department rate method.

9. One of the necessary conditions that indicates that the single plantwide factory overhead rate may lead to product cost distortion is _____ in production department factory overhead rates.

10. One of the necessary conditions that indicates that the single plantwide factory overhead rate may lead to product cost distortion is differences in the _____ of allocation-base usage.

11. Under activity-based costing, factory overhead costs are first accounted for in activity cost _____.

12. Product L is set up 12 times, with each production run consisting of 10 units. If the setup activity rate is $400 per setup, then the setup cost per unit is _____.

13. The activity pool for the purchasing activity is $360,000, while there are 12,000 purchase orders estimated for the period; thus, the purchasing activity rate is _____.

14. Under activity-based costing, more factory overhead will be allocated to a(n) _____ product.

15. Under activity-based costing, an activity base used for the quality control inspection activity would be _____ _____ _____.

16. Under generally accepted accounting principles, selling and administrative expenses should be treated as _____ expenses; however, management may wish to treat them as _____ costs for management reporting purposes.

17. The traditional method of allocating selling and administrative expenses to products is based on product _____ volumes.

18–19. Product K had 150 sales orders and 10 returns, while Product L had 200 sales orders and 50 returns. The activity rate for the sales order processing activity is $36 per sales order, while the activity rate for the return processing activity is $145 per return.

18. The sales order and return processing activity cost of Product K is _____.

19. The sales order and return processing activity cost of Product L is _____.

20. Activity-based costing could be used by a hospital to determine the cost of services consumed by a(n) _____.

FILL IN THE BLANK—Part B

Instructions: Answer the following questions or complete the statements by writing the appropriate words or amounts in the answer blanks.

1. An accounting framework based on relating the cost of activities to final products is called _____-_____ _____.

2. The single plantwide factory overhead rate method's greatest advantage is _____.

3. Each department under the multiple production department rate method uses _____ (the same or different) factory overhead rates.

4. In activity-based costing, activity rates are determined by dividing the cost budgeted for each activity by an estimated _____ _____.

5. Under the single plantwide rate method, the total factory overhead allocated to products will be _____ (less than, equal to, or greater than) the total factory overhead allocated under the multiple production department rate method.

6. A method of allocating factory overhead to products by using factory overhead rates for each production department is termed the

   _____ _____ _____ _____ method.

7. A method of allocating factory overhead to products by using a single factory overhead rate is termed the _____ _____ _____ method.

8. A(n) _____ _____ _____ activates an administrative process to change the product design characteristics.

9. The activity of changing the characteristics of a machine to prepare for manufacturing a different product is termed a(n) _____.

10. The denominator used to determine a production department rate is termed a(n) _____ _____.

11–14. In each of the following independent cases assume a multiple-department, multi-product factory. Answer "yes" if using a plantwide factory overhead rate would likely distort product costs and "no" if it would not.

11. The factory overhead rates in Departments A and B are both $40 per machine hour. _____

12. The factory overhead rate in Department T is $32 per machine hour, in Department V it is $62 per machine hour, and the products use the same number of hours in each department. _____

13. One product consumes 12 direct labor hours at $18 per direct labor hour in Department L and 8 direct labor hours at $40 per direct labor hour in Department M. Another product consumes 6 direct labor hours at $18 per direct labor hour in Department L and 15 direct labor hours at $40 per hour in Department M. _____

14. One product consumes 20 direct labor hours at $30 per direct labor hour in Department D and 12 direct labor hours at $30 per direct labor hour in Department E. Another product consumes 12 direct labor hours at $30 per direct labor hour in Department D and 20 direct labor hours at $30 per hour in Department E. _____

15. The danger of product cost distortion is that it can lead to bad decisions and flawed _____.

16. If the reaction activity cost is estimated to be $850,000 for the year and the reactor is expected to run for 2,000 hours during the year, the activity rate per machine hour is _____.

17. Product T requires 12 hours in the Reaction Department. The reaction activity cost allocated to Product T using the activity rate in Question 16 is _____.

18. If the budgeted factory overhead is $1,400,000 and the direct labor hours budgeted is 50,000, the plantwide factory overhead rate per direct labor hour is _____.

19. Selling and administrative activities _____ (can or cannot) be allocated to products for management reporting purposes.

20. An appropriate activity base for the radiological testing activity in a hospital is _____ _____ _____.

MULTIPLE CHOICE

Instructions: Circle the best answer for each of the following questions.

1. Which of the following allocation bases would most likely be used under the single plantwide rate method?
   a. total direct labor hours
   b. number of setups
   c. number of engineering changes
   d. Packing Department direct labor hours

2. Hy-Gain Company manufactures two products—cellular phones and pagers. The budgeted factory overhead for Hy-Gain for the next period is $450,000. Hy-Gain expects to operate the plant for 10,000 machine hours during the next period. The cellular phone requires 1.2 machine hours, and the pager requires 0.8 machine hours. How much factory overhead per unit should be allocated to the pager under the single plantwide rate method?
   a. $36.00
   b. $45.00
   c. $54.00
   d. $56.25

3. Celebration Cards Inc. is a greeting card company that uses the multiple production department rate method to allocate factory overhead. Celebration Cards prints cards for two occasions—Valentine's Day and birthdays. The cards are manufactured through two departments—Printing and Cutting. The Printing Department has a factory overhead budget of $120,000 and 5,000 machine hours. The Cutting Department has a factory overhead budget of $80,000 and 8,000 direct labor hours. If a case of Valentine's Day cards requires 0.5 machine hours in the Printing Department and 0.25 direct labor hours in the Cutting Department, how much factory overhead should be allocated to the case?
   a. $11.55
   b. $12.00
   c. $14.50
   d. $15.40

4. Activity-based costing will generally have _____ activity (allocation) rates than the multiple production department rate method.

   a. fewer

   b. more

   c. the same number of

   d. either fewer or more

5. The multiple production department rate method will lead to more accurate factory overhead allocation than the single plantwide rate method when:

   a. there are significant differences between the production department rates

   b. there are differences in the ratios of allocation-base usage of the products across the departments

   c. either a or b

   d. both a and b

6. The activity rate is determined by dividing the estimated activity cost pool by:

   a. the activity-base usage quantity

   b. the total estimated activity base

   c. the total estimated allocation base

   d. the units of production

7. Luv 'N Stuff Company manufactures stuffed toy animals. Activities and the activity rates from the selling and administrative expenses include the following:

   Sales order processing .... $45 per sales order
   Customer service .... $125 per request
   Customer return processing .... $400 per returned item

   How much selling and administrative expense should be allocated to the Benny the Bear toy if Benny had 60 sales orders, 5 customer requests for service, and 4 customer returns?

   a. $4,925

   b. $39,330

   c. $5,200

   d. $2,700

8. When should selling and administrative expenses be allocated using the relative sales volume method?

   a. when these expenses are proportional to sales volume

   b. never

   c. when sales are expected to be nearly the same for each product

   d. when these expenses are not proportional to sales volume

9–10. Portions of the Central Railroad Company's costs consist of crew salaries, fuel, and railcar loading and unloading. These costs are estimated for the year to be as follows:

Crew salaries	$360,000
Fuel	80,000
Railcar loading and unloading	290,000

In addition, the Central Railroad Company estimates that their trains pull 2,900 railcars over the year. The trains will run a total of 25,000 miles. Train 102 consists of 60 railcars moved from Cincinnati to Kansas City—a distance of 550 miles.

9. What is the activity rate for "railcar loading and unloading"?

   a. $35 per railcar

   b. $75 per railcar

   c. $100 per railcar

   d. $11.60 per mile

10. What is the crew salary, fuel, and railcar loading and unloading cost for Train 102?

   a. $15,103

   b. $15,680

   c. $16,060

   d. $30,880

TRUE/FALSE

Instructions: Indicate whether each of the following statements is true or false by placing a check mark in the appropriate column.

	True	False
1. The advantage of the single plantwide factory overhead rate method is that it is simple to use.	____	____
2. The production department overhead cost under the multiple production department rate method must be the same as a production activity pool under activity-based costing.	____	____
3. The multiple production department rate method will lead to improved factory overhead cost allocation only if there are significant rate differences between the production departments..	____	____
4. The activity-based costing method uses activity pools to allocate factory overhead to products.	____	____
5. Activity-based costing should only be used by manufacturing companies.	____	____

	True	False

6. An example of an activity is the plant manager's salary...... ____ ____

7. Engineering change orders are issued to change engineering personnel. .... ____ ____

8. Activity-based costing will lead to more accurate factory overhead allocations when products exhibit complexity that is unrelated to production volumes............................. ____ ____

9. Selling and administrative expenses allocated to products under the relative sales volume method is based on the assumption that these expenses are proportional to sales volume. .... ____ ____

10. Service companies should not allocate overhead since they do not have product costs for determining inventory... ____ ____

EXERCISE 23-1

Peacock Apparel Company manufactures three styles of men's shirts: casual, work, and dress. The company has budgeted the following overhead expenses for the upcoming period:

Factory depreciation	$ 40,000
Indirect labor	840,000
Factory electricity	90,000
Indirect materials	70,000
Selling expenses	350,000
Administrative expenses	170,000
Total	$1,560,000

Factory overhead is allocated to the three products on the basis of direct labor hours. The products had the following production budget volume and direct labor hours per unit information:

	Budgeted Production Volume	Direct Labor Hours per Unit
Casual	450,000	0.1
Work	200,000	0.2
Dress	150,000	0.3
	800,000	

Instructions

(1) Determine the single plantwide factory overhead rate.

(2) Use the factory overhead rate in (1) to determine the amount of total and per-unit factory overhead allocated to each of the three products under generally accepted accounting principles.

EXERCISE 23-2

Sure-Stop Brake Company produces three types of brakes: auto, truck, and bus. A brake is first pressed in the Press Department. The pressed brakes are then sent to the Cure Department, where the final brake is cured for strength. Sure-Stop uses the multiple production department rate method of allocating factory overhead costs. Sure-Stop's factory overhead costs are budgeted as follows:

Press Department overhead	$600,000
Cure Department overhead	240,000
Total	$840,000

The machine hours estimated for each production department are as follows:

	Press Department	Cure Department	Total
Machine hours	8,000	24,000	32,000

Machine hours are used to allocate the production department overhead to the products. The machine hours per set for each product for each production department were obtained from the engineering records as follows:

	Auto Brake	Truck Brake	Bus Brake
Press Department	0.30	0.5	1
Cure Department	2.25	2.5	3
Machine hours per brake set	2.55	3.0	4

Instructions

(1) Determine the production department factory overhead rates.

(2) Use the production department factory overhead rates to determine the factory overhead per set for each product.

_____

_____

_____

_____

_____

_____

_____

_____

_____

_____

_____

_____

_____

_____

_____

EXERCISE 23-3

Perfect Reflection Printer Company is estimating the activity cost associated with producing laser and ink jet printers. The indirect labor can be traced to four separate activity pools, based on time records provided by the indirect employees. The budgeted activity cost and activity-base information is provided below.

Activity	Activity Cost Pool	Activity Base
Purchasing	$225,000	Number of purchase orders
Inspecting	140,000	Number of inspections
Materials handling	70,000	Number of moves
Product development	165,000	Number of engineering change orders
Total	$600,000	

Estimated activity-base usage and unit information for Perfect Reflection's two product lines was determined from corporate records as follows:

	Number of Purchase Orders	Number of Inspections	Number of Moves	Number of Engineering Changes	Units
Laser printer	4,000	5,500	20,000	800	4,000
Ink jet printer	6,000	1,500	15,000	200	4,000
Totals	10,000	7,000	35,000	1,000	8,000

Instructions

(1) Determine the activity rate for each activity cost pool.

(2) Determine the total and per-unit activity-based cost for each product.

PROBLEM 23-1

Bon Voyage Luggage Company manufactures two products: suitcases and garment bags. The factory overhead is incurred as follows:

Indirect labor	$ 800,000
Cutting Department	800,000
Assembly Department	200,000
Total	$1,800 000

The activity base associated with the two production departments is direct labor hours. The indirect labor can be assigned to two different activities, as follows

Activity	Activity Cost Pool	Activity Base
Inspection	$600,000	Number of inspections
Setup	200,000	Number of setups
Total	$800,000	

The activity-base information for the two products is shown below.

	Number of Inspections	Number of Setups	Dir. Labor Hours— Cutting	Dir. Labor Hours— Assembly	Units Produced
Suitcase	1,000	200	8,000	2,000	10,000
Garment bag	3,000	600	2,000	8,000	10,000
Totals	4,000	800	10,000	10,000	20,000

Instructions

(1) Determine the factory overhead rates under the multiple production department rate method. Assume that indirect labor is associated with the production departments, so that the total factory overhead is $1,200,000 and $600,000 for Cutting and Assembly, respectively.

(2) Determine the total and per-unit factory overhead costs allocated to each product using the multiple production department overhead rates in (1).

(3) Determine the activity rates, assuming that the indirect labor is associated with activities rather than with the production departments.

(4) Determine the total and per-unit factory overhead costs assigned to each product under activity-based costing.

(5) Explain the difference in the per-unit factory overhead allocated to each product under the multiple production department rate and activity-based costing methods.

PROBLEM 23-2

XCell Soft Inc. sells commercial software. The company incurs selling and administrative expenses of $21,600,000. The company wishes to assign these costs to its three major products: integrated accounting software, human resource (HR) software, and project management software. These expenses are related to three major activities: 1-800 customer support, customer return processing, and order processing. The activity cost pool and activity bases associated with these activities are provided below.

Activity	Activity Cost Pool	Activity Base
1-800 customer support	$ 5,400,000	Number of calls
Customer return processing	7,200,000	Number of returns
Order processing	9,000,000	Number of sales orders
Total	$21,600,000	

The following activity-base usage and units sold information for the three products is available from the corporate records:

	Integrated Accounting	Human Resource	Project Management	Total
Number of 1-800 calls	20,000	20,000	10,000	50,000
Number of returns	2,000	5,000	5,000	12,000
Number of orders	20,000	15,000	10,000	45,000
Unit volume	50,000	40,000	10,000	100,000

In addition, the price and the cost of goods sold per unit for the three products are as follows:

	Per Unit
Price	$500
Cost of goods sold	50
Gross profit	$450

Instructions

(1) Determine the activity rates for each of the three activity pools.

(2) Determine the activity costs allocated to the three products using the activity rates in (1).

(3) Construct product profitability reports for the three products using the activity costs in (2). The reports should disclose the gross profit and operating profit associated with each product.

(4) Provide recommendations to management based on the profit reports in (3).

24

Cost Management for Just-in-Time Manufacturers

QUIZ AND TEST HINTS

The following hints may be helpful to you in preparing for a quiz or a test over the material covered in Chapter 24.

1. This chapter has two major sections: the just-in-time philosophy and the impact of the just-in-time philosophy on management accounting. You should expect multiple-choice questions about the just-in-time philosophy. In addition, you may be asked to compare and contrast the just-in-time philosophy with traditional manufacturing approaches.

2. Be prepared to define and calculate the lead time for a product.

3. You should be able to provide some simplified journal entries for a just-in-time manufacturer. In addition, you may have multiple-choice or short-answer questions asking you to identify the unique features of management accounting in a just-in-time environment.

4. Be prepared to answer multiple-choice questions about quality cost definitions. In addition, be able to prepare a cost of quality report, a Pareto chart of quality costs, and a value-added/nonvalue-added analysis.

5. The specialized terms associated with a just-in-time environment are introduced in this chapter. You should be prepared to answer true/false or multiple-choice questions about these terms. As a review of the key terms, do the Matching Exercise on page 1040.

FILL IN THE BLANK—Part A

Instructions: Answer the following questions or complete the statements by writing the appropriate words or amounts in the answer blanks.

1. Another term for lean (or short-cycle) manufacturing is _____-____-_____ _____.

2. A company embracing just-in-time manufacturing will _____ (reduce or increase) inventory.

3. _____ _____ is a measure of the time that elapses between starting a unit of product into the beginning of a process and completing the unit of product.

4. The amount of lead time associated with actually converting materials to a finished unit is called _____-_____ _____ _____.

5. Long setup times result in larger inventories and longer _____ _____.

6–7. A batch of 50 units of a product moves sequentially through three machining operations that require 16 minutes per unit of total machine time. The total time to move the batch between the three machines is 12 minutes.

6. The total value-added lead time is _____.

7. The total nonvalue-added lead time is _____.

8. The effort necessary to change a machine's characteristics to prepare for production of a new product is termed a(n) _____.

9. A(n) _____-_____ _____ occurs when work is organized around processes.

10. Allowing employees to evaluate each other is an example of _____ _____.

11. Pull manufacturing uses _____ to signal production quantities to be used by the next stage of production.

12. Entering into long-term supplier agreements is an example of _____ _____.

13–14. A product cell has budgeted conversion costs of $175,000 for the month. The cell is planned to be available for 250 hours during the month. Each unit requires 9 minutes in the cell. The materials cost is $110 per unit.

13. The budgeted conversion cost per unit is _____.

14. The cost debited to Raw and In Process Inventory for the period is _____.

15. Support resources in a just-in-time manufacturer are often
_____ (allocated or directly assigned) to product
cells.

16. Lead time, percent good quality, and orders filled on time are examples of
_____ performance measures.

17. The budgeted cell conversion rate for a cell with a budgeted cost of
$430,000 for 860 planned hours of production is _____.

18. The cost associated with correcting defects discovered by the customer is
called a(n) _____ _____ cost.

19. A(n) _____ _____ is a graphical approach to identifying
important problems or issues.

20. The cost of activities that are necessary to meet customer requirements,
such as product design and conversion activities, are called _____-
_____ activity costs.

FILL IN THE BLANK—Part B

Instructions: Answer the following questions or complete the statements by
writing the appropriate words or amounts in the answer blanks.

1. A business philosophy that focuses on eliminating time, cost, and poor
quality within manufacturing and nonmanufacturing processes is called
_____-____-_____ _____.

2. The production approach based on producing goods to finished goods
inventory rather than producing goods to fill a customer order is called
_____ _____ _____.

3. The production scheduling approach in which work in process flows
through the factory based on the actual demand of the customer is called
_____ manufacturing.

4. A layout of the factory in which production processes are organized
around product cells is called a(n) _____-_____
layout.

5. The time a product waits or moves unnecessarily is called
_____-_____ _____ _____.

6–7. A batch of 24 units of a product moves sequentially through three machining operations that require 28 minutes per unit of total machine time. The
total time to move the batch between the three machines is 15 minutes.

6. The total value-added lead time is _____.

7. The total nonvalue-added lead time is _____.

8. A bar chart that shows the totals of a particular attribute for a number of categories is a(n) _____ _____.

9. The accounting system in a just-in-time environment will frequently use a combined account for _____ and _____ ____ _____.

10. Employees that can perform multiple operations within a product cell are said to be _____-_____.

11. _____ _____ _____ is a method of using computers to electronically communicate orders, relay information, and make or receive payments from one organization to another.

12–13. A product cell has budgeted conversion costs of $360,000 for the month. The cell is planned to be available for 240 hours during the month. Each unit requires 18 minutes in the cell. The materials cost is $75 per unit.

12. The budgeted conversion cost per unit is _____.

13. The cost debited to Raw and In Process Inventory for the period is _____.

14. If $18,200 was budgeted to support 260 hours of production, the cell conversion cost rate would be _____.

15. Performance measures for a just-in-time manufacturer often include both financial and _____ measures.

16. The costs associated with correcting defects prior to shipment to a customer is called _____ _____ costs.

17. Employee training is an example of the _____ quality cost classification.

18. The cost of activities that are not required by the customer, such as errors, omissions, and failures, are called _____-_____ activity costs.

19. The relationship between the costs of quality is such that increasing investments in prevention and appraisal activities should reduce the cost of _____ and _____ activities.

20. A(n) _____ _____ _____ _____ identifies the activity cost associated with each quality cost classification and the percentage of total quality costs associated with each classification.

MULTIPLE CHOICE

Instructions: Circle the best answer for each of the following questions.

1. Which of the following is not a characteristic of just-in-time manufacturing?
    a. emphasizes pull manufacturing
    b. emphasizes a process-oriented layout
    c. reduces inventory
    d. reduces setup time

2. Which of the following is the best approach for reducing lead time?
    a. supplier partnering
    b. employee involvement
    c. reducing setup time
    d. electronic data interchange

3. Which of the following would be considered value-added lead time?
    a. setup time
    b. move time
    c. waiting in inventory
    d. machine time

4. If a product is manufactured in batch sizes of 20 units and has two operations, and it takes 2 minutes to manufacture each unit, what is the within-batch wait time?
    a. 38 minutes
    b. 40 minutes
    c. 76 minutes
    d. 80 minutes

5. A company using a just-in-time manufacturing system will likely debit materials purchases to:
    a. Raw and In Process Inventory
    b. Materials Inventory
    c. Work in Process Inventory
    d. Cost of Goods Sold

6–7. The cell rate is $175 per hour. Each unit has $48 per unit of materials cost and requires 18 minutes of cell conversion time. The cell produces 300 units, of which 285 are sold.

6. What is the debit to Raw and In Process Inventory?
    a. $14,400
    b. $15,750
    c. $30,150
    d. $66,900

7. What is the Finished Goods Inventory balance?

   a. $3,345

   b. $1,507.50

   c. $787.50

   d. $720

8. Which of the following is an example of external failure cost?

   a. scrap

   b. rework

   c. billing errors and correction

   d. quality control inspection

9. The purpose of a Pareto chart is to:

   a. visually highlight important categories

   b. provide trend information

   c. summarize profitability

   d. visually demonstrate how two variables are related to each other

10. An activity analysis shows the following quality cost activities:

Warranty	$100,000
Rework	80,000
Final inspection	30,000
Supplier certification	60,000
Employee training	90,000
Disposal of scrap	40,000
Total	$400,000

    What is the percentage of prevention cost to total cost?

    a. 32.5%

    b. 37.5%

    c. 45%

    d. 47.5%

TRUE/FALSE

Instructions: Indicate whether each of the following statements is true or false by placing a check mark in the appropriate column.

	True	False
1. Just-in-time manufacturing is primarily an inventory reduction technique.	____	____
2. Lead time is equivalent to the amount of standard direct labor time needed to produce a product.	____	____
3. A product-oriented layout reduces the amount of materials movement.	____	____
4. Reducing setup time will increase within-batch wait time.	____	____
5. Pull manufacturing uses kanbans to signal materials movement and release.	____	____
6. A JIT environment will increase the number of accounting and control transactions due to kanbans.	____	____
7. JIT accounting combines materials and work in process into a single account.	____	____
8. JIT manufacturing often increases the need for cost allocation.	____	____
9. Prevention costs are value-added activities.	____	____
10. A Pareto chart is a line chart plotting quality costs over time.	____	____

EXERCISE 24-1

Twin Image Scanner Company is considering a new just-in-time product cell. The present manufacturing approach produces a scanner in four separate process steps. The production batch sizes are 40 units. The process time for each process step is as follows:

Process Step 1: 3 minutes   Process Step 3: 12 minutes
Process Step 2: 7 minutes   Process Step 4: 5 minutes

The time required to move each batch between each of the production steps is 15 minutes. In addition, the time to move raw materials to process step 1 and to move completed units from process step 4 to finished goods inventory is also 15 minutes each.

The new just-in-time layout will allow the company to reduce the batch sizes from 40 units to 3 units. The time required to move each batch between the production steps and inventory locations will be reduced to 5 minutes. The processing time in each process step will stay the same.

Instructions: Determine the value-added, nonvalue-added, and total lead times under the present and proposed production approaches.

EXERCISE 24-2

Clarity Audio Inc. uses a just-in-time strategy to manufacture CD players. The company manufactures CD players through a single product cell. The budgeted conversion cost for the year is $1,845,000 for 2,050 production hours. Each unit requires 10 minutes of cell process time. During April, 1,025 CD players are manufactured in the cell. The estimated materials cost per unit is $135. The following summary transactions took place during March:

a. Materials are purchased to manufacture April production.

b. Conversion costs were applied to production.

c. 1,025 CD players are assembled and placed in finished goods.

d. 1,000 CD players are sold for $480 per unit.

Instructions

(1) Determine the budgeted cell conversion cost per hour.

(2) Determine the budgeted cell conversion cost per unit.

(3) Journalize the summary transactions (a)–(d) for April, using the journal provided on the next page.

_____

_____

_____

_____

_____

_____

_____

_____

_____

_____

_____

_____

_____

_____

_____

_____

_____

_____

_____

_____

_____

JOURNAL   PAGE

	DATE		DESCRIPTION	POST. REF.	DEBIT	CREDIT	
1							1
2							2
3							3
4							4
5							5
6							6
7							7
8							8
9							9
10							10
11							11
12							12
13							13
14							14
15							15
16							16
17							17
18							18
19							19
20							20

EXERCISE 24-3

Veracity Instruments Inc. manufactures instrument panels for the automotive industry. An activity analysis was conducted, and the following activity costs were identified with the manufacture and sale of instrument panels:

Activity	Activity Cost
Emergency equipment maintenance	$ 70,000
Employee training	15,000
Correcting shipment errors	25,000
Warranty claims	190,000
Final inspection	50,000
Supplier development	5,000
Processing customer returns	140,000
Scrap reporting	22,000
Disposing of scrap	160,000
Inspecting materials	40,000
Preventive equipment maintenance	10,000
Total	$727,000

Instructions: Prepare a Pareto chart of these activities.

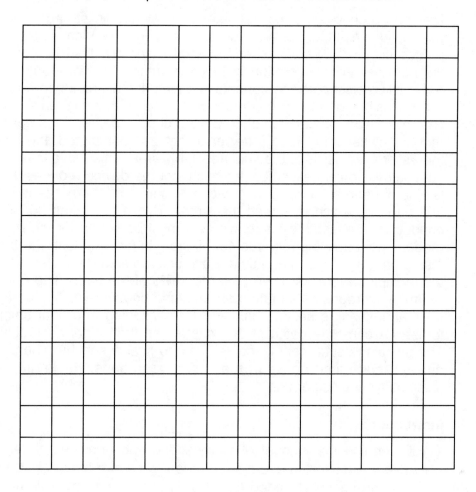

PROBLEM 24-1

Memory Technologies Inc. manufactures electronic storage devices for computers, such as magnetic and optical drives. The manufacturing process includes printed circuit (PC) card assembly, final assembly, testing, and shipping. The PC card assembly operation includes a number of individuals responsible for assembling electronic components into the printed circuit boards. Each operator is responsible for soldering components according to a given set of instructions. Operators work on batches of 80 printed circuit boards. Each board requires 12 minutes of assembly time. After each batch is completed, the operator moves the assembled cards to the final assembly area. This move takes 10 minutes to complete. The final assembly for each storage device requires 18 minutes and is also done in batches of 80 devices. A batch of 80 devices is moved into the test building, which is across the street. This move takes 30 minutes. Before conducting the test, the test equipment must be set up for the particular device model. The test setup requires 45 minutes. In the final test, the 80-unit batch is tested one circuit board at a time. Each test requires 4 minutes. On average, the test equipment breaks down (fails) for 10% of the tests. The equipment maintenance averages 10 minutes per machine breakdown. The completed batch, after all testing, is sent to shipping for packaging and final shipment to customers. A complete batch of 80 units is sent from final assembly to shipping. The shipping department is located next to final assembly. Thus, there is insignificant move time between these two operations. Packaging and labeling requires 4 minutes per unit.

Instructions

(1) Determine the amount of value-added and nonvalue-added lead time in this process for an average storage device in a batch of 80 units. Categorize the nonvalue-added time into wait, move, and equipment breakdown time.

(2) How could this process be improved so as to reduce the amount of waste in the process?

_____

_____

_____

_____

_____

_____

_____

_____

_____

_____

_____

PROBLEM 24-2

The president of Kokimo Company has been concerned about the growth in costs over the last several years. The president asked the controller to perform an activity analysis to gain a better insight into these costs. The activity analysis revealed the following:

Activity	Activity Cost
Preventive machine maintenance	$ 45,000
Disposing of scrap	125,000
Correcting invoice errors	30,000
Fina! inspection	38,000
Expediting production	65,000
Disposing of materials with poor quality	45,000
Responding to customer quality complaints	120,000
Inspecting work in process	22,000
Producing product	200,000
Inspecting materials	10,000
Total	$700,000

The production process is complicated by quality problems, requiring the production manager to expedite production and dispose of scrap.

Instructions

(1) Prepare a Pareto chart of the company's quality cost-related activities.

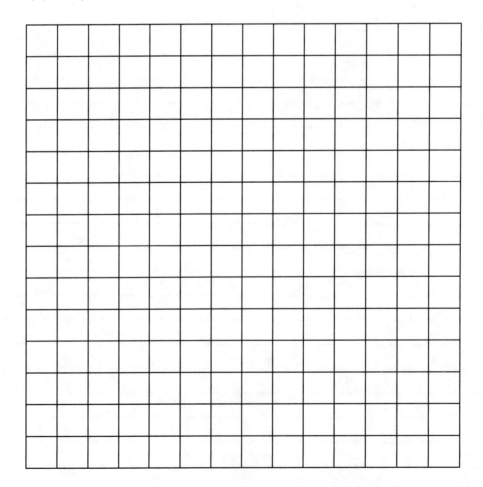

(2) Use the activity cost information to determine the percentage of total quality costs that are prevention, appraisal, internal failure, and external failure.

(3) Determine the percentage of total quality costs that are value- and nonvalue-added.

(4) Interpret the information.

_____

_____

_____

_____

_____

_____

_____

_____

_____

_____

_____

_____

_____

_____

_____

_____

_____

_____

_____

_____

_____

_____

_____

_____

_____

_____

_____

_____

_____

Statement of Cash Flows

QUIZ AND TEST HINTS

The following hints may be helpful to you in preparing for a quiz or a test over the statement of cash flows.

1. Study the new terminology introduced in this chapter for possible use in fill-in-the-blank, multiple-choice, or true/false questions. As a review of the key terms, do the Matching Exercise in the text.

2. You should be able to classify different types of cash flows as operating, investing, or financing activities. Test questions on this material often appear in a true/false or multiple-choice format.

3. Instructors may emphasize the indirect method, the direct method, or both methods of preparing the statement of cash flows. Adjust your studying to the method or methods that your instructor emphasized during class lectures and in homework assignments. You should be able to prepare a statement of cash flows using one or both methods. Often, instructors will include a partially completed statement of cash flows on an examination and require students to complete it. The Illustrative Problem is a good study aid for both the indirect and direct methods.

4. The work sheets for preparing the statement of cash flows appear in the Appendix to the chapter. Study the Appendix if your instructor has expressed a preference for use of the work sheet in preparing the statement of cash flows.

FILL IN THE BLANK—Part A

Instructions: Answer the following questions or complete the statements by writing the appropriate words or amounts in the answer blanks.

1. The financial statement that reports a firm's major cash inflows and outflows for a period is the _____ _____ _____ _____.

2. The two alternative methods of reporting operating activities in the statement of cash flows are the _____ and _____ methods.

3–7. Indicate the section of the statement of cash flows in which each of the following would appear (answer operating activities, investing activities, or financing activities):

3. Depreciation expense on equipment would appear under _____ activities.

4. Sale of long-term investments would appear under _____ activities.

5. Sale of equipment would appear under _____ activities.

6. Issuance of bonds would appear under _____ activities.

7. Sale of patents would appear under _____ activities.

8–10. This year, Young Company issued 500,000 shares of common stock, inventory increased by $20,000, and a new asset was purchased for $1,000,000. For each of these events, indicate whether net cash flows increased or decreased:

8. Common stock issued. Net cash flows _____.

9. Inventory increased. Net cash flows _____.

10. New asset purchased. Net cash flows _____.

11. Cash dividends of $35,000 were declared during the year. Cash dividends payable were $8,000 and $8,750 at the beginning and end of the year, respectively. The amount of cash flows for payment of dividends during the year is _____.

12. The net income from operations was $75,000, and the only revenue or expense item not affecting cash was depreciation expense of $27,000. The amount of net cash flows from operating activities that would appear on the statement of cash flows is _____.

13. A corporation purchased and retired 3,000 shares of its $50 par common stock, originally issued at par, for $65. Cash flows amounted to _____.

14. If a fixed asset having a book value of $54,000 is sold (for cash) at a gain of $6,000, the total amount reported as a cash flow is _____.

15. The $47,000 net income for the year included a loss of $2,500 on the sale of land. Exclusive of the effect of other adjustments, the amount of net cash flows from operating activities is _____.

16. A corporation issued $1,000,000 of bonds payable at 104. Cash flow from this transaction was _____.

17. If 15,000 shares of $20 par common stock were issued at 22, the amount to be reported in the cash flows from financing activities section of the statement of cash flows would be _____.

18. Cash flows resulting from the redemption of debt securities are classified in the statement of cash flows as related to _____ activities.

19. Jones Company had cash flow from operations of $75,000. This year, dividends paid amounted to $6,000, and the company purchased $9,000 in spare parts for machines used on the factory floor. Jones Company's free cash flow is _____.

20. A cash flow term for which an amount should not be reported in the financial statements because it could mislead readers is _____ _____ _____ _____.

FILL IN THE BLANK—Part B

Instructions: Answer the following questions or complete the statements by writing the appropriate words or amounts in the answer blanks.

1. The _____ method of analyzing operating cash flows begins with net income and adjusts it for revenues and expenses that do not involve the receipt or payment of cash.

2. The statement of cash flows groups cash flow activities as financing, investing, or _____.

3. When the _____ method of reporting cash flows is used, a supplemental schedule reconciling net income and net cash flow from operating activities must also be prepared.

4–8. Indicate the section of the statement of cash flows in which each of the following would appear (answer operating activities, investing activities, or financing activities):

4. Retirement of long-term debt would appear under _____ activities.

5. Sale of common stock would appear under _____ activities.

6. Net income would appear under _____ activities.

7. Payment of cash dividends would appear under _____ activities.

8. Purchase of equipment would appear under _____ activities.

9. _____ investing and financing activities that will affect future cash flows are reported in a separate schedule to the statement of cash flows.

10–11. Indicate whether each of the following items would be added to or deducted from net income on the schedule reconciling net income with cash flows from operating activities:

10. Increase in inventories would be _____ _____ net income.

11. Increase in accounts payable would be _____ _____ net income.

12. If a loss of $15,000 is incurred in selling (for cash) store equipment having a book value of $345,000, the total amount reported as a cash flow is _____.

13. A corporation issued $750,000 of 20-year bonds at 99½. Cash flows were _____.

14. A corporation purchased 25,000 shares of its $100 par common stock, originally issued at par, as treasury stock for $125. Cash flows were _____.

15. Cash dividends of $50,000 were declared during the year. Cash dividends payable were $8,500 and $12,500 at the beginning and end of the year, respectively. The amount of cash flows for the payment of dividends during the year is _____.

16. The net loss from operations was $15,000, and the only revenue or expense item not affecting cash was depreciation expense of $35,000. The amount to be reported as net cash flow from operating activities on the statement of cash flows is _____.

17. In preparing a statement of cash flows under the indirect method, it is efficient to analyze the _____ _____ account first.

18. The $55,000 net income for the year included a gain of $4,000 on the sale of equipment. Exclusive of the effect of other adjustments, the amount of net cash flows from operating activities is _____.

19. Cash flow for interest expense is included on the statement of cash flows as an _____ activity.

20. A measure of cash available for corporate purposes, after productive assets are maintained and the business owners are paid dividends, is called _____ _____ _____.

MULTIPLE CHOICE

Instructions: Circle the best answer for each of the following questions.

1. Which of the following is not one of the major types of cash flow activities that are reported on the statement of cash flows?

   a. cash flows from financing activities

   b. cash flows from selling activities

   c. cash flows from operating activities

   d. cash flows from investing activities

2. Noncash investing and financing activities which may have a significant effect on future cash flows are reported:

   a. in the statement of cash flows

   b. in a separate schedule to accompany the statement of cash flows

   c. in the retained earnings statement

   d. in a footnote accompanying the balance sheet

3. Under the indirect method, which of the following items must be deducted from reported net income to determine net cash flow from operating activities?

   a. depreciation of fixed assets

   b. decreases in current assets

   c. decreases in current liabilities

   d. loss on sale of equipment

4. During the past year, Lockhart Inc. declared $40,000 in cash dividends. If the beginning and ending balance of the dividends payable account was $12,000 and $10,000, respectively, what amount of cash paid for dividends will appear in the cash flow from financing activities section of the statement of cash flows?

   a. $30,000

   b. $38,000

   c. $40,000

   d. $42,000

5. Under the direct method, which of the following items must be added to operating expenses reported on the income statement to determine cash payments for operating expenses?

   a. increase in accrued expenses

   b. decrease in prepaid expenses

   c. increase in income taxes payable

   d. increase in prepaid expenses

6. An example of a cash flow from a financing activity is:
   a. receipt of cash from sale of land
   b. receipt of cash from collection of accounts receivable
   c. payment of cash for acquisition of treasury stock
   d. payment of cash for new machinery

7. Which of the following items appears first on the statement of cash flows prepared using the direct method?
   a. retained earnings
   b. cash received from customers
   c. net income
   d. depreciation

8. Which of the following would not be considered a noncash investing and financing activity in preparing a statement of cash flows?
   a. withdrawal of cash by the owner of a business
   b. issuance of common stock to retire long-term debt
   c. acquisition of a manufacturing plant by issuing bonds
   d. issuance of common stock in exchange for convertible preferred stock

9. To convert the cost of merchandise sold as reported on the income statement to cash payments for merchandise, the cost of merchandise sold is increased for the:
   a. increase in inventories
   b. increase in accounts payable
   c. decrease in inventories
   d. decrease in accounts receivable

10. Cash payments for income taxes are included on the statement of cash flows as:
    a. financing activities
    b. investing activities
    c. operating activities
    d. nonoperating activities

TRUE/FALSE

Instructions: Indicate whether each of the following statements is true or false by placing a check mark in the appropriate column.

		True	**False**
1.	The statement of cash flows is required as part of the basic set of financial statements.	_____	_____
2.	Cash outflows from the payment of cash dividends is a type of financing activity.	_____	_____
3.	Cash receipts from the sale of fixed assets would be classified as a cash flow from investing activities.	_____	_____
4.	Under the direct method, depreciation is the first noncash account balance analyzed.	_____	_____
5.	Under the indirect method, increases in current liabilities are deducted from net income reported on the income statement in determining cash flows from operating activities.	_____	_____
6.	Noncash investing and financing activities that may have a significant effect on future cash flows should be included in a separate schedule to the statement of cash flows.	_____	_____
7.	The correct amount to include in cash flows from financing activities is cash dividends paid, not cash dividends declared.	_____	_____
8.	The analysis of retained earnings provides the starting point for determining cash flows from operating activities under the indirect method only.	_____	_____
9.	The direct method provides a more accurate figure of cash flows from operating activities than does the indirect method.	_____	_____
10.	Under the direct method, the increase in the trade receivables account is deducted from sales to determine the cash received from customers.	_____	_____

EXERCISE 1

Instructions: Listed in the first column below are selected transactions and account balance changes of Mason Inc. for the current year. Indicate by placing a check mark in the appropriate column(s) how each of the items would be reported in the statement of cash flows.

Item	Cash Flows From			Schedule of Noncash Investing and Financing Activities
	Operating Activities	Investing Activities	Financing Activities	
1. Decrease in prepaid expenses				
2. Retirement of bonds				
3. Proceeds from sale of investments ...				
4. Increase in inventories				
5. Issuance of common stock				
6. Purchase of equipment				
7. Cash dividends paid				
8. Acquisition of building in exchange for bonds				
9. Amortization of patents				
10. Amortization of discount on bonds payable				

EXERCISE 2

The net income reported on the income statement of Hunter Inc. for the current year was $150,000. Depreciation recorded on equipment and building amounted to $45,000 for the year. Balances of the current asset and current liability accounts at the beginning and end of the year are as follows:

	End of Year	Beginning of Year
Cash	$ 42,875	$ 36,250
Trade receivables (net)	147,500	137,500
Inventories	109,375	93,750
Prepaid expenses	9,250	11,875
Accounts payable (merchandise creditors)	57,000	40,000
Salaries payable	7,625	10,625

Instructions: Prepare the cash flows from operating activities section of the statement of cash flows using the indirect method.

EXERCISE 3

The income statement of Hunter Inc. for the current year is as follows:

Sales		$530,000
Cost of merchandise sold		130,000
Gross profit		$400,000
Operating expenses:		
Depreciation expense	$ 45,000	
Other operating expenses	160,000	
Total operating expenses		205,000
Income before income tax		$195,000
Income tax		45,000
Net income		$150,000

Instructions: Using the income statement presented above and the account balances provided in Exercise 2, prepare the cash flows from operating activities section of the statement of cash flows using the direct method.

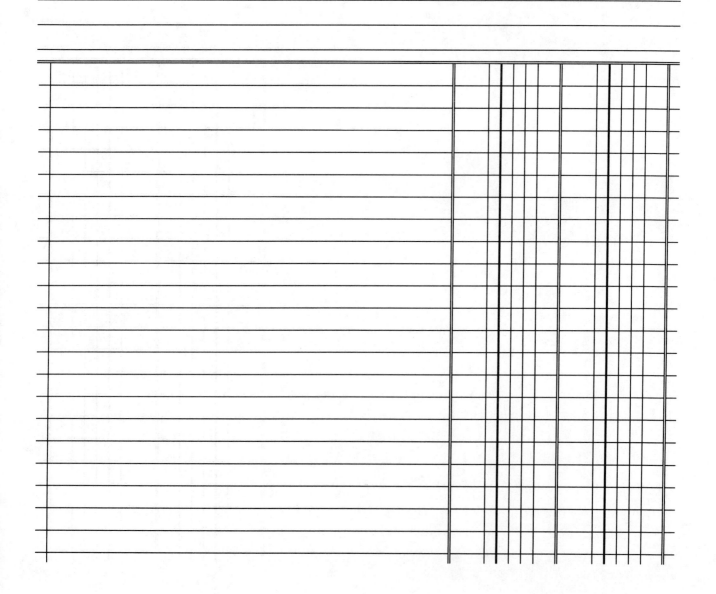

PROBLEM 1

The comparative balance sheet of Stellar Inc. at December 31, 2001, appears below.

Stellar Inc.
Comparative Balance Sheet
December 31, 2001 and 2000

	2001	2000	Increase Decrease*
Assets			
Cash	$ 84,000	$ 66,000	$ 18,000
Trade receivables (net)	156,000	144,000	12,000
Inventories	300,000	306,000	6,000*
Prepaid expenses	12,000	14,400	2,400*
Land	80,000	96,000	16,000*
Building	360,000	360,000	0
Accumulated depreciation—building	(120,000)	(91,200)	(28,800)
Equipment	180,000	102,000	78,000
Accumulated depreciation—equipment	(72,000)	(70,800)	(1,200)
Total assets	$980,000	$926,400	$ 53,600
Liabilities			
Accounts payable	$216,000	$208,800	$ 7,200
Dividends payable	24,000	21,600	2,400
Bonds payable	240,000	300,000	60,000*
Total liabilities	$480,000	$530,400	$ 50,400*
Stockholders' Equity			
Common stock	$140,000	$120,000	$ 20,000
Retained earnings	360,000	276,000	84,000
Total stockholders' equity	$500,000	$396,000	$104,000
Total liabilities and stockholders' equity	$980,000	$926,400	$ 53,600

The following additional data were taken from the records of Stellar Inc.:

a. Equipment costing $96,000 was purchased, and fully depreciated equipment costing $18,000 was discarded.
b. Net income, including gain on sale of land, was $114,000. Depreciation expense on equipment was $19,200; on building, $28,800.
c. Bonds payable of $60,000 were retired at face value.
d. A cash dividend of $30,000 was declared.
e. Land costing $36,000 was sold for $54,000, resulting in an $18,000 gain on the sale.
f. Land was acquired by issuing common stock, $20,000.

Instructions: Complete the following statement of cash flows using the indirect method of reporting cash flows from operating activities.

Stellar Inc.
Statement of Cash Flows
For Year Ended December 31, 2001

Cash flows from operating activities:

Net income, per income statement .... $ _____

Add: Depreciation .... $ _____

Decrease in inventories ....   _____

Decrease in prepaid expenses ....   _____

Increase in accounts payable ....   _____   _____

                                                            $ _____

Deduct: Increase in trade receivables .... $ _____

Gain on sale of land ....   _____   _____

Net cash flow from operating activities .... $ _____

Cash flows from investing activities:

Cash received from land sold .... $ _____

Less cash paid for purchase of equipment ....   _____

Net cash flow used for investing activities .....   _____

Cash flows from financing activities:

Cash used to retire bonds payable .... $ _____

Cash paid for dividends ....   _____

Net cash flow used for financing activities .....   _____

Increase in cash .... $ _____

Cash, January 1, 2001 ....   _____

Cash, December 31, 2001 .... $ _____

Schedule of Noncash Investing and Financing Activities:

Acquisition of land by issuance of common stock .... $ _____

PROBLEM 2

The income statement of Stellar Inc. is provided below. Stellar's comparative balance sheet data were provided in Problem 1.

Instructions: Complete the statement of cash flows for Stellar Inc. using the direct method of reporting cash flows from operating activities.

Stellar Inc.
Income Statement
For Year Ended December 31, 2001

Sales		$575,000
Cost of merchandise sold		225,000
Gross profit		$350,000
Operating expenses:		
Depreciation expense	$ 48,000	
Other operating expenses	172,000	
Total operating expenses		220,000
Income from operations		$130,000
Other income:		
Gain on sale of land		18,000
Income before income tax		$148,000
Income tax		34,000
Net income		$114,000

Stellar Inc.
Statement of Cash Flows
For Year Ended December 31, 2001

Cash flows from operating activities:

    Cash received from customers .... $ _____

    Deduct: Cash payments for merchandise ...... $ _____

        Cash payments for operating
        expenses .... _____

        Cash payments for income tax .... _____ _____

    Net cash flow from operating activities .... $ _____

Cash flows from investing activities:

    Cash received from land sold .... $ _____

    Less cash paid for purchase of equipment .... _____

    Net cash flow used for investing activities ..... _____

Cash flows from financing activities:

    Cash used to retire bonds payable .... $ _____

    Cash paid for dividends .... _____

    Net cash flow used for financing activities ..... _____

Increase in cash .... $ _____

Cash, January 1, 2001 .... _____

Cash, December 31, 2001 .... $ _____

Schedule of Noncash Investing and Financing Activities:

    Acquisition of land by issuance of common stock .... $ _____

Schedule Reconciling Net Income with Cash Flows from Operating Activities:

    Net income, per income statement .... $ _____

    Add: Depreciation .... $ _____

        Decrease in inventories .... _____

        Decrease in prepaid expenses .... _____

        Increase in accounts payable .... _____ _____

                                           $ _____

    Deduct: Increase in trade receivables .... $ _____

        Gain on sale of land .... _____ _____

    Net cash flow provided by operating activities .... $ _____

Financial Statement Analysis

QUIZ AND TEST HINTS

The following hints may be helpful to you in preparing for a quiz or a test over financial statement analysis.

1. When studying financial statement analysis, you should focus primarily on the various analytical measures described and illustrated. These measures are also summarized in the text. Pay special attention to each measure's computation, its use, and its classification as either a solvency or profitability measure. A good study aid for the computation of the measures is the Illustrative Problem.

2. Instructors often use true/false and multiple-choice questions to test this material. Such questions may require the computation of ratios or test your understanding of various terms. As a review of the key terms, do the Matching Exercise in the text.

FILL IN THE BLANK—Part A

Instructions: Answer the following questions or complete the statements by writing the appropriate words or amounts in the answer blanks.

1. Percentage analysis used to show the relationship of the component parts to the total in a single statement is called _____ _____.

2. _____ _____ focuses primarily on the relationship between operating results as reported in the income statement and resources available to the business as reported in the balance sheet.

3. The use of ratios showing the ability of an enterprise to pay its current liabilities is known as _____ _____ _____.

4. _____ is the ability of a business to meet its financial obligations as they come due.

5. _____-_____ statements are prepared in order to compare percentages of the current period with past periods, to compare individual businesses, or to compare one business with industry percentages published by trade associations or financial information services.

6. The ratio of current assets to current liabilities is called the _____ ratio.

7. The ratio of _____ _____ _____ _____ is a profitability measure that shows how effectively a firm utilizes its assets.

8. The ratio of the sum of cash, receivables, and marketable securities to current liabilities is called the _____-_____ ratio.

9. _____ _____ _____ _____ _____ _____ is the ratio of net income available to common shareholders to the number of common shares outstanding.

10. The excess of the current assets of a business over its current liabilities is called _____ _____.

11. _____ _____ _____ is computed by dividing net sales on account by the average net accounts receivable.

12. _____ _____ is computed by dividing the cost of goods sold by the average inventory.

13. The ratio of _____ _____ _____ _____ is a solvency measure that indicates the margin of safety for creditors.

14. The number of times _____ _____ _____ _____ is a measure of the risk that dividends to preferred stockholders may not be paid.

15. If significant amounts of nonoperating income and expense are reported on the income statement, it may be desirable to compute the ratio of _____ _____ _____ to total assets as a profitability measure.

16. The rate earned on _____ _____ focuses only on the rate of profits earned on the amount invested by common stockholders.

17. Earnings per share and _____ per share on common stock are commonly used by investors in assessing alternative stock investments.

18. All publicly held corporations are required to have a(n) _____ _____ of their financial statements.

19. The ratio of _____ _____ _____ _____-_____ _____ is a solvency measure that indicates the margin of safety of the noteholders or bondholders.

20. In a vertical analysis of the income statement, each item is stated as a percent of _____ _____.

FILL IN THE BLANK—Part B

Instructions: Answer the following questions or complete the statements by writing the appropriate words or amounts in the answer blanks.

1. The percentage analysis of increases and decreases in corresponding items in comparative financial statements is called _____ _____.

2. The _____ _____ is a profitability measure that shows the rate of return to common stockholders in terms of cash dividend distributions.

3. The _____ _____ report describes the results of an independent examination of the financial statements.

4. The _____ _____ _____ _____ _____ _____ is computed by dividing the net accounts receivable at the end of the year by the average daily sales on account.

5. The _____ _____ _____ _____ _____ _____ is computed by dividing the inventory at the end of the year by the average daily cost of goods sold.

6. The number of times _____ _____ _____ is a measure of the risk that interest payments will not be made if earnings decrease.

7. The _____ _____ _____ _____ _____ measures the profitability of total assets, without considering how the assets are financed.

8. The _____ _____ _____ _____ _____ is computed by dividing net income by average total stockholders' equity.

9. The difference between the rate earned by a business on the equity of its stockholders and the rate earned on total assets is called _____.

10. The _____-_____ ratio is computed by dividing the market price per share of common stock at a specific date by the annual earnings per share.

11. The _____ _____ section of a corporate annual report normally includes a statement that the financial statements are management's responsibility and that they have been prepared according to generally accepted accounting principles.

12. _____ _____ are cash and other current assets that can be quickly converted to cash.

13. In a _____-_____ statement, all items are expressed as percentages.

14. _____ _____ focuses on the ability of a business to pay or otherwise satisfy its current and noncurrent liabilities.

15. The current ratio is sometimes called the working capital ratio or the _____ ratio.

16. Two measures that are useful for evaluating the management of inventory are the inventory turnover and the _____ _____ _____ _____ _____ _____.

17. A profitability measure often quoted in the financial press and normally reported in the income statement in corporate annual reports is _____ _____ _____.

18. All items in _____-_____ statements are expressed only in relative terms.

19. Quick assets normally include cash, marketable securities, and _____.

20. Management's assessment of the company's internal accounting control system normally is provided in the _____ _____ section of the corporate annual report.

MULTIPLE CHOICE

Instructions: Circle the best answer for each of the following questions.

1. Statements in which all items are expressed only in relative terms (percentages of a common base) are:

   a. relative statements

   b. horizontal statements

   c. vertical statements

   d. common-size statements

2. Which one of the following measures is a solvency measure?

   a. rate earned on total assets

   b. price-earnings ratio

   c. accounts receivable turnover

   d. ratio of net sales to assets

3. Based on the following data for the current year, what is the inventory turnover?
   Net sales, $6,500,000
   Cost of goods sold, $4,000,000
   Inventory, beginning of year, $250,000
   Inventory, end of year, $345,000
   Accounts receivable, beginning of year, $175,000
   Accounts receivable, end of year, $297,000

   a. 26.7

   b. 16

   c. 13.4

   d. 11.6

4. Based on the following data for the current year, what is the accounts receivable turnover?
   Net sales on account, $6,500,000
   Cost of goods sold, $4,000,000
   Inventory, beginning of year, $250,000
   Inventory, end of year, $345,000
   Accounts receivable, beginning of year, $175,000
   Accounts receivable, end of year, $297,000

   a. 37.1

   b. 27.5

   c. 21.8

   d. 17

5. Which of the following sections of corporate annual reports normally includes a statement concerning an assessment of a company's internal accounting control system?

   a. financial highlights section

   b. president's letter

   c. independent auditors' report

   d. management report

6. A measure used in evaluating the efficiency in collecting receivables is:

   a. working capital ratio

   b. quick ratio

   c. receivables/inventory ratio

   d. number of days' sales in receivables

7. Based on the following data for the current year, compute the number of times interest charges are earned:
   Income before income tax, $510,000
   Interest expense, $30,000
   Total assets, $4,080,000

   a. 8

   b. 17

   c. 18

   d. 136

8. Based on the following data for the current year, what is the quick ratio?
   Cash, $27,000
   Marketable securities, $23,000
   Receivables, $90,000
   Inventory, $105,000
   Current liabilities, $70,000

   a. 2.0

   b. 3.5

   c. 0.7

   d. 1.5

9. In vertical analysis of the balance sheet, each asset item is stated as a percent of total:

   a. current assets

   b. assets

   c. current liabilities

   d. liabilities

10. Based on the following data for the current year, what is the earnings per share on common stock?
Net income, $460,000
Preferred dividends, $50,000
Interest expense, $24,000
Shares of common stock outstanding, 50,000

   a. $9.20

   b. $8.68

   c. $8.20

   d. $7.72

TRUE/FALSE

Instructions: Indicate whether each of the following statements is true or false by placing a check mark in the appropriate column.

		True	False
1.	In horizontal analysis of the income statement, each item is stated as a percentage of total sales.	___	___
2.	Solvency is the ability of a business to meet its financial obligations as they come due.	___	___
3.	The ratio of (net sales to assets) provides a solvency measure that shows the margin of safety of the debtholders.	___	___
4.	The acid-test ratio or quick ratio is the ratio of the sum of cash, receivables, and marketable securities to current liabilities.	___	___
5.	Net sales on account divided by the year-end net accounts receivable gives the accounts receivable turnover.	___	___
6.	Net income minus the amount required for preferred dividends divided by the average common stockholders' equity gives the rate earned on common stockholders' equity.	___	___
7.	The rate earned on total assets is calculated by subtracting interest expense from net income and dividing this sum by the average total assets.	___	___
8.	The tendency on the rate earned on stockholders' equity to vary disproportionately from the rate earned on total assets is referred to as financial leverage.	___	___
9.	A profitability measure that shows the rate of return to common stockholders in terms of cash dividends is known as the dividend yield on common stock.	___	___
10.	The excess of the current assets of an enterprise over its current liabilities and stockholders' equity is called working capital.	___	___

EXERCISE 1

Instructions: Using the condensed income statement information presented below, perform a vertical analysis for Delta Corp. for the years ending December 31, 2000 and 1999, stating each item as a percent of revenues.

	2000	Percent	1999	Percent
Revenues	$450,000		$389,000	
Costs and expenses:				
Cost of sales	$200,000		$176,000	
Selling and administrative expenses	100,000		73,000	
Interest expense	250		396	
Total costs and expenses	$300,250		$249,396	
Earnings before income taxes	$149,750		$139,604	
Income taxes	35,321		33,765	
Net earnings	$114,429		$105,839	

EXERCISE 2

Instructions: Using the condensed balance sheet data presented below, perform a horizontal analysis for Carson Inc. on December 31, 2000. Indicate the amount and percent increase (decrease) in the columns provided.

			Increase (Decrease)	
	2000	1999	Amount	Percent
Current assets	$250,000	$219,500		
Fixed assets	435,000	401,600		
Intangible assets	42,000	46,500		
Current liabilities	88,000	80,000		
Long-term liabilities	225,000	250,000		
Common stock	214,000	167,600		
Retained earnings	200,000	170,000		

PROBLEM 1

Instructions: Using the information below and on the following page, perform a horizontal analysis for Nordic Inc. by filling in the Amount and Percent columns that are provided. (Round all percents to one decimal place.)

Nordic Inc.
Comparative Income Statement
For the Years Ended December 31, 2000 and 1999

	2000	1999	Increase (Decrease) Amount	Increase (Decrease) Percent
Sales	$690,500	$585,000		
Sales returns and allowances	25,500	23,000		
Net sales	$665,000	$562,000		
Cost of goods sold	420,000	330,000		
Gross profit	$245,000	$232,000		
Selling expenses	$ 43,000	$ 47,700		
Administrative expenses	31,000	31,000		
Total operating expenses	$ 74,000	$ 78,700		
Operating income	$171,000	$153,300		
Other income	13,000	16,400		
	$184,000	$169,700		
Other expense	58,000	53,500		
Income before income taxes	$126,000	$116,200		
Income taxes	34,000	32,400		
Net income	$ 92,000	$ 83,800		

Nordic Inc.
Comparative Balance Sheet
December 31, 2000 and 1999

Assets	2000	1999	Increase (Decrease) Amount	Percent
Cash	$ 76,000	$ 69,000		
Marketable securities	98,900	130,000		
Accounts receivable (net)	199,000	195,000		
Inventory	450,000	375,000		
Prepaid expenses	28,000	26,300		
Long-term investments	35,000	35,000		
Fixed assets (net)	871,000	835,000		
Intangible assets	18,000	22,800		
Total assets	$1,775,900	$1,688,100		
Liabilities				
Current liabilities	$ 129,000	$ 107,000		
Long-term liabilities	420,000	440,000		
Total liabilities	$ 549,000	$ 547,000		
Stockholders' Equity				
Preferred 3% stock, $100 par	$ 102,000	$ 93,000		
Common stock, $50 par	549,900	530,100		
Retained earnings	575,000	518,000		
Total stockholders' equity	$1,226,900	$1,141,100		
Total liabilities and stockholders' equity	$1,775,900	$1,688,100		

PROBLEM 2

Instructions: Using the information below and on the following page, perform a vertical analysis for Voyageur Inc. by filling in the Percent columns on the statements provided. (Round all percents to one decimal place.)

Voyageur Inc.
Comparative Balance Sheet
December 31, 2000 and 1999

	2000		1999	
Assets	Amount	Percent	Amount	Percent
Cash	$ 500,000		$ 425,000	
Marketable securities	200,000		185,000	
Accounts receivable (net)	680,000		575,000	
Inventory	860,000		740,000	
Prepaid expenses	104,000		95,000	
Long-term investments	450,000		410,000	
Fixed assets	6,556,000		5,420,000	
Total assets	$9,350,000	100%	$7,850,000	100%
Liabilities				
Current liabilities	$1,090,000		$1,050,000	
Long-term liabilities	2,150,000		2,050,000	
Total liabilities	$3,240,000		$3,100,000	
Stockholders' Equity				
Preferred 5% stock, $100 par	$ 350,000		$ 350,000	
Common stock, $10 par	2,550,000		2,550,000	
Retained earnings	3,210,000		1,850,000	
Total stockholders' equity	$6,110,000		$4,750,000	
Total liabilities and stockholders' equity	$9,350,000	100%	$7,850,000	100%

Voyageur Inc.
Income Statement
For the Year Ended December 31, 2000

	Amount	Percent
Sales	$12,800,000	
Sales returns and allowances	300,000	
Net sales	$12,500,000	100%
Cost of goods sold	7,550,000	
Gross profit	$ 4,950,000	
Selling expenses	$ 1,550,000	
Administrative expenses	825,000	
Total operating expenses	$ 2,375,000	
Operating income	$ 2,575,000	
Other income	125,000	
	$ 2,700,000	
Other expense (interest)	150,000	
Income before income taxes	$ 2,550,000	
Income taxes	937,000	
Net income	$ 1,613,000	

PROBLEM 3

Voyageur Inc. declared $250,000 of common stock dividends during 2000. The price of Voyageur's common stock on December 31, 2000 is $29.75.

Instructions: Using the data for Voyageur Inc. from Problem 2, determine the following amounts and ratios for 2000. (Round all ratios to one decimal point.)

		Calculation	Final Result
a.	Working capital		
b.	Current ratio		
c.	Acid-test ratio		
d.	Accounts receivable turnover		
e.	Number of days' sales in receivables		
f.	Inventory turnover		
g.	Number of days' sales in inventory		
h.	Ratio of fixed assets to long-term liabilities		
i.	Ratio of liabilities to stockholders' equity		

	Calculation	Final Result
j. Number of times interest charges earned		
k. Number of times preferred dividends earned		
l. Ratio of net sales to assets		
m. Rate earned on total assets		
n. Rate earned on stockholders' equity		
o. Rate earned on common stockholders' equity		
p. Earnings per share on common stock		
q. Price-earnings ratio		
r. Dividends per share of common stock		
s. Dividend yield		

Solutions

CHAPTER 14

Fill In the Blank—Part A

1. financial
2. staff
3. cost
4. direct labor
5. factory overhead
6. conversion
7. job order
8. crediting, debiting
9. time tickets
10. allocation
11. $41.67
12. activity-based
13. overapplied (or overabsorbed)
14. rate
15. cost of goods sold
16. materials requisitions
17. stock ledger
18. period
19. administrative
20. service

Fill In the Blank—Part B

1. managerial
2. line
3. controller
4. direct materials
5. indirect labor
6. product prices
7. debited, credited
8. requisitions
9. job cost
10. time tickets
11. activity driver
12. $5,625
13. $66
14. work in process
15. underapplied (or underabsorbed)
16. time tickets
17. finished goods
18. $100,975
    {[($175,000 / 20,000)
    × (12,000 − 3,500)]
    + $26,600}
19. selling
20. cost of services

Multiple Choice

1.	b	6.	c
2.	d	7.	c
3.	b	8.	a
4.	d	9.	c
5.	b	10.	a

True/False

1.	T	6.	T
2.	F	7.	F
3.	F	8.	T
4.	T	9.	F
5.	F	10.	T

Exercise 14-1

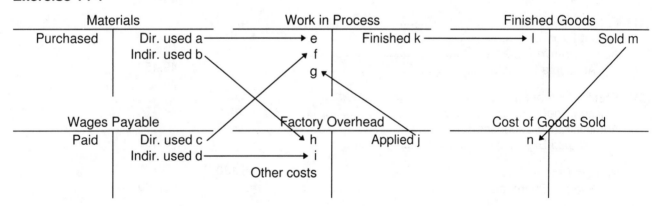

Exercise 14-2

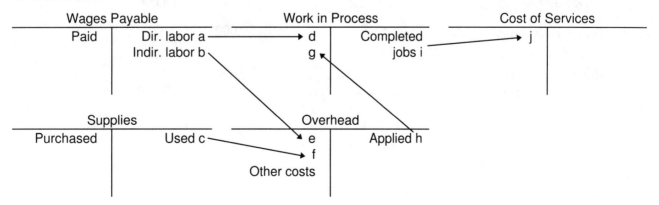

Exercise 14-3

(a) $3.25 per machine hour   ($65,000 / 20,000 hours)

(b) 42% of direct labor cost   ($243,600 / $580,000)

(c)

Work in Process—Factory 1	5,850	
Factory Overhead—Factory 1		5,850
($3.25 × 1,800)		
Work in Process—Factory 2	20,370	
Factory Overhead—Factory 2		20,370
(42% × $48,500)		

(d) Factory 1—$200 debit (underapplied)
Factory 2—$270 credit (overapplied)

Problem 14-1

(1)	Materials	60,000	
	Prepaid Expenses	5,300	
	Accounts Payable		65,300
(2)	Work in Process	23,200	
	Factory Overhead	1,200	
	Materials		24,400
(3)	Work in Process	35,900	
	Factory Overhead	2,700	
	Wages Payable		38,600
(4)	Factory Overhead	12,200	
	Selling Expenses	21,950	
	Administrative Expenses	15,300	
	Accounts Payable		49,450
(5)	Factory Overhead	5,000	
	Selling Expenses	800	
	Administrative Expenses	600	
	Prepaid Expenses		6,400
(6)	Work in Process	25,130	
	Factory Overhead		25,130
(7)	Finished Goods	53,000	
	Work in Process		53,000
(8)	Accounts Receivable	160,000	
	Sales		160,000
	Cost of Goods Sold	110,000	
	Finished Goods		110,000

Problem 14-2

Cash			
Bal.	135,400	(1)	78,000
		(4)	12,500

Finished Goods		
Bal.	50,800	
(6)	164,000	

Work in Process			
Bal.	33,800	(6)	164,000
(2)	56,000		
(3)	70,000		
(5)	24,000		

Materials			
Bal.	18,000	(2)	58,400
(1)	78,000		

Factory Overhead			
Bal.	3,000	(5)	24,000
(2)	2,400		
(3)	5,000		
(4)	12,500		

Wages Payable		
	(3)	75,000

CHAPTER 15

Fill In the Blank—Part A

1. job order
2. process
3. factory overhead
4. allocating
5. physical
6. credited
7. units to be assigned costs
8. 34,500   (58,500 − 24,000)
9. equivalent
10. 18,300   [(8,000 × 60%) + (18,500 − 8,000) + (7,500 × 40%)]
11. $98,820   ($32,500 + $66,320)
12. $56,700   ($5.40 × 10,500)
    ($98,820 / 18,300 = $5.40 per unit)
    (18,500 − 8,000 = 10,500; the units started and completed)
13. $16,200   ($5.40 × 7,500 × 40%)
14. cost per equivalent unit
15. $531.25   ($68,000 / 128)
16. 18,600   (solve for $99,510 / X = $5.35)
17. cost of production
18. yield
19. just-in-time
20. manufacturing cells

Fill In the Blank—Part B

1. process
2. job order
3. department
4. direct labor, factory overhead
5. conversion
6. fifo (first-in, first-out)
7. partially completed
8. ending in-process inventory
9. 600
10. whole
11. March
12. evenly
13. 510
14. $25
15. 8,800
16. multiplying
17. $10,350
18. $1,590
19. $11,940
20. kanbans

Multiple Choice

1. c		6. c	
2. d		7. d	
3. a		8. b	
4. b		9. d	
5. a		10. c	

True/False

1. T		6. T	
2. T		7. T	
3. T		8. F	
4. F		9. F	
5. F		10. F	

Exercise 15-1

(a) Purchases
(b) Direct materials
(c) Direct labor
(d) Indirect materials
(e) Factory overhead applied
(f) Costs transferred out/Costs transferred in
(g) Direct labor
(h) Factory overhead applied
(i) Costs transferred out/Costs transferred in
(j) Cost of goods sold

Exercise 15-2

Units	Total Whole Units	% Material to be Completed in April	% Conversion to be Completed in April	(1) Equivalent Units for Materials	(2) Equivalent Units for Conversion
Beginning Inventory	12,000	0%	70%	0	8,400
Started and Completed (66,000 – 12,000)	54,000	100%	100%	54,000	54,000
Transferred Out	66,000			54,000	62,400
Ending Inventory	8,000	100%	20%	8,000	1,600
Total Equivalent Units to Account for				62,000	64,000

Costs		(3) Direct Materials	(4) Conversion Costs	Total
Total Costs Incurred this Period		$148,800	$326,400	
Cost per Equivalent Unit		$2.40 ($148,800 ÷ 62,000)	$5.10 ($326,400 ÷ 64,000)	
Beginning Inventory—Balance				$ 32,600
Beginning Inventory—Completed (equiv. units × rate)		0	$ 42,840	42,840
Started and Completed (equiv. units × rate)		$129,600	275,400	405,000
Transferred Out	(6)			$480,440
Ending Inventory (equiv. units × rate)	(5)	$ 19,200	$ 8,160	27,360
Total Costs Charged to Department				$507,800

Problem 15-1

(1) Materials 210,000
      Accounts Payable 210,000

(2) Factory Overhead—Department 10 2,100
    Factory Overhead—Department 20 600
    Work in Process—Department 10 18,000
    Work in Process—Department 20 24,000
      Materials 44,700

(3)	Factory Overhead—Department 10	2,700	
	Factory Overhead—Department 20	2,700	
	Work in Process—Department 10	25,000	
	Work in Process—Department 20	20,000	
	Wages Payable		50,400
(4)	Factory Overhead—Department 10	1,500	
	Factory Overhead—Department 20	2,250	
	Accounts Payable		3,750
(5)	Factory Overhead—Department 10	4,200	
	Factory Overhead—Department 20	3,150	
	Accumulated Depreciation—Fixed Assets		7,350
(6)	Work in Process—Department 10	25,500	
	Work in Process—Department 20	15,000	
	Factory Overhead—Department 10		25,500
	Factory Overhead—Department 20		15,000
(7)	Work in Process—Department 20	68,500	
	Work in Process—Department 10		68,500
(8)	Finished Goods	115,000	
	Work in Process—Department 20		115,000
(9)	Accounts Receivable	160,000	
	Sales		160,000
	Cost of Goods Sold	122,000	
	Finished Goods		122,000

Problem 15-2

Ivy Inc.
Cost of Production Report—Polishing Department
For the Month Ended March 31, 20--

		Equivalent Units	
Units	Whole Units	Direct Materials	Conversion
Units charged to production:			
Inventory in process, March 1	5,000		
Received from Cutting	21,000		
Total units accounted for by Polishing Dept.	26,000		
Units to be assigned costs:			
Inventory in process, March 1 (30% completed)	5,000	0	3,500
Started and completed in March	15,000	15,000	15,000
Transferred to finished goods in March	20,000	15,000	18,500
Inventory in process, March 31 (60% completed)	6,000	6,000	3,600
Total units to be assigned cost	26,000	21,000	22,100

Ivy Inc.
Cost of Production Report—Polishing Department (Concluded)
For the Month Ended March 31, 20--

| | Costs | | |
Costs	Direct Materials	Conversion	Total Costs
Unit costs:			
Total cost for March in Polishing	$105,000	$296,140	
Total equivalent units (from above)	÷ 21,000	÷ 22,100	
Cost per equivalent unit	$ 5.00	$ 13.40	
Costs charged to production:			
Inventory in process, March 1			$ 37,025
Costs incurred in March			401,140
Total costs accounted for by Polishing Dept.			$438,165
Costs allocated to completed and partially completed units:			
Inventory in process, March 1—balance			$ 37,025
To complete inventory in process, March 1	$ 0	$ 46,900 (a)	46,900
Started and completed in March	75,000 (b)	201,000 (c)	276,000
Transferred to finished goods in March			$359,925
Inventory in process, March 31	30,000 (d)	48,240 (e)	78,240
Total costs assigned by Polishing Dept.			$438,165

(a)   3,500 × $13.40 = $46,900
(b) 15,000 × $5.00 = $75,000
(c) 15,000 × $13.40 = $201,000
(d)   6,000 × $5.00 = $30,000
(e)   3,600 × $13.40 = $48,240

CHAPTER 16

Fill In the Blank—Part A

1. activity bases (or activity drivers)
2. relevant range
3. variable costs
4. fixed
5. mixed
6. mixed
7. direct costing
8. cost-volume-profit
9. contribution margin ratio
10. 9,500
11. increase
12. increase
13. 7,500
14. break-even
15. horizontal
16. profit-volume
17. "what if" analysis (or sensitivity analysis)
18. sales mix
19. margin of safety
20. operating leverage

Fill In the Blank—Part B

1. activity drivers
2. variable costs
3. fixed
4. fixed costs
5. mixed
6. semifixed
7. variable cost per unit
8. contribution margin
9. profit-volume ratio
10. contribution margin
11. fixed costs
12. break-even point
13. increase
14. decrease
15. decrease
16. sales, costs
17. sensitivity analysis
18. sales mix
19. 4
20. straight lines

Multiple Choice

1. d
2. c
3. b
4. c
5. b
6. a
7. a
8. c
9. d
10. b
11. c
12. d

True/False

1. T
2. F
3. T
4. F
5. T
6. T
7. F
8. F
9. F
10. T

Exercise 16-1

(1)   Difference in total costs: $300,000   ($550,000 − $250,000)
Difference in total units of production:
      30,000 units   (50,000 units − 20,000 units)

(2)   Variable cost per unit: $10 ($300,000 / 30,000 units)
Fixed cost estimated at highest level of production:
      Total Cost = Total Variable Cost + Fixed Cost
      $550,000 = ($10 × 50,000 units) + Fixed Cost
      $550,000 = $500,000 + Fixed Cost
      Fixed Cost = $50,000
                or
Fixed Cost estimated at lowest level of production:
      Total Cost = Total Variable Cost + Fixed Cost
      $250,000 = ($10 × 20,000 units) + Fixed Cost
      $250,000 = $200,000 + Fixed Cost
      Fixed Cost = $50,000

(3)   Total Cost = Total Variable Cost + Fixed Cost
      Total Cost = ($10 × 80,000 units) + $50,000
      Total Cost = $800,000 + $50,000
      Total Cost = $850,000

Exercise 16-2

Chart: Cost-Volume-Profit Chart
(a)   fixed costs
(b)   break-even point
(c)   operating profit area
(d)   total sales
(e)   operating loss area
(f)   total costs

Exercise 16-3

(1)   ($2,000,000 − $1,700,000) / $2,000,000 = 15%

(2)   ($150,000 − $100,000) / $150,000 = 33%

(3) $300,000 / $175,000 = 1.71

(4)   Sales $700,000
      Variable costs   300,000
      Contribution margin $400,000
      $400,000 / $200,000 = 2

Problem 16-1

(1) $700,000 / $50 = 14,000 units

(2) $710,000 / $50 = 14,200 units

(3) $700,000 / $49 = 14,286 units

(4) $700,000 / $52 = 13,462 units

(5)   ($700,000 + $300,000) / $50 = 20,000 units

Problem 16-2

(1)   ($180 × .80) + ($280 × .20) = $200 unit selling price of E
($140 × .80) + ($190 × .20) = $150 unit variable cost of E
($40 × .80) + ($90 × .20) = $50 unit contribution margin of E
Break-even point (units): $400,000 / $50 = 8,000 units
Sales necessary in dollars: 8,000 × $200 = $1,600,000

(2)

	Product A	Product B	Total
Sales:			
6,400 units × $180	$1,152,000		$1,152,000
1,600 units × $280		$448,000	448,000
Total sales	$1,152,000	$448,000	$1,600,000
Variable costs:			
6,400 units × $140	896,000		896,000
1,600 units × $190		304,000	304,000
Total variable costs	$ 896,000	$304,000	$1,200,000
Contribution margin			$ 400,000
Fixed costs			400,000
Operating profit			0

CHAPTER 17

Fill In the Blank—Part A

1. absorption
2. manufacturing margin
3. less than
4. fixed factory overhead
5. $18,000, greater than
6. $60,000 (12,000 × $5)
7. controllable costs
8. sales mix
9. $800,000 (20,000 × $40)
10. $1,370,000 [(8,000 × $40) + (15,000 × $70)]
11. $182,000 (3,500 × $52)
12. $196,000 (3,500 × $56)
13. $450,000
14. $101,250
15. $303,750
16. $86,250
17. price factor
18. $23,250 decrease in variable cost of goods sold
19. $10,000 increase in variable cost of goods sold
20. increase

Fill In the Blank—Part B

1. absorption costing
2. contribution margin
3. gross profit
4. variable cost of goods sold
5. absorption
6. product
7. variable
8. absorption
9. included
10. excluded
11. $189,000
12. $308,000
13. $63,000
14. $53,000
15. $415,000 (5,000 × $83)
16. $455,000 (5,000 × $91)
17. quantity factor
18. $8,000 increase in variable cost of goods sold
19. $12,500 decrease in variable cost of goods sold

Multiple Choice

1. c
2. c
3. a
4. b
5. b*
6. b**
7. b
8. a
9. a
10. b

True/False

1. F
2. T
3. F
4. F
5. T
6. F
7. T
8. F
9. T
10. F

* (20,000 + 15,000) × $32
** (15,000 × $32) + (11,000 × $65)

Exercise 17-1

(1)

Power Racquet Inc.
Absorption Costing Income Statement
For the Month Ended March 31, 20--

Sales (42,000 units × $45)	$1,890,000
Cost of goods sold (42,000 units × $26)	1,092,000
Gross profit	$ 798,000
Selling and administrative expenses ($210,000 + $160,000)	370,000
Income from operations	$ 428,000

(2)

Power Racquet Inc.
Variable Costing Income Statement
For the Month Ended March 31, 20--

Sales		$1,890,000
Variable cost of goods sold (42,000 units × $18)		756,000
Manufacturing margin		$1,134,000
Variable selling and administrative expenses		210,000
Contribution margin		$ 924,000
Fixed costs:		
Fixed manufacturing costs	$360,000	
Fixed selling and administrative expenses	160,000	520,000
Income from operations		$ 404,000

(3) The difference between the absorption and variable costing income from operations of $24,000 ($428,000 − $404,000) can be explained as follows:

Change in inventory	3,000
Fixed overhead per unit	× $8.00
Income from operations difference	$24,000

Under absorption costing, the fixed manufacturing cost included in the cost of goods sold is matched with the revenues. As a result, 3,000 units that were produced but unsold (inventory) include fixed manufacturing cost, which is not included in the cost of goods sold. Under variable costing, all of the fixed manufacturing cost is deducted in the period in which it is incurred, regardless of the amount of the inventory change. Thus, when the inventory increases, the absorption costing income statement will have a higher income from operations than will the variable costing income statement.

Exercise 17-2

Jupiter Company
Variable Costing Income Statement
For the Month Ended May 31, 20--

Sales (46,000 units)		$650,000
Variable cost of goods sold:		
Variable cost of goods manufactured	$210,000 [1]	
Less inventory, May 31 (4,000 units)	16,800 [2]	
Variable cost of goods sold		193,200
Manufacturing margin		$456,800
Variable selling and administrative expenses		84,000
Contribution margin		$372,800
Fixed costs:		
Fixed manufacturing costs	$140,000	
Fixed selling and administrative expenses	61,000	201,000
Income from operations		$171,800

[1] $350,000 − $140,000 (total manufacturing cost less fixed manufacturing cost)
[2] $210,000 / $350,000 × $28,000 = $16,800 (the ratio of variable to total manufacturing costs times the value of the ending inventory under absorption costing) *OR* $210,000 / 50,000 units manufactured = $4.20; $4.20 × 4,000 units = $16,800

Exercise 17-3

(1)

Snow Glide Company
Contribution Margin by Sales Territory

	Eastern	Western
Sales	$19,000,000	$18,000,000
Variable cost of goods sold	12,000,000	10,000,000
Manufacturing margin	$ 7,000,000	$ 8,000,000
Selling expenses	5,000,000	5,000,000
Contribution margin	$ 2,000,000	$ 3,000,000
Contribution margin ratio	10.5%	16.7%

(2) The contribution margin ratios for the Alpine and Nordic skis are different. Alpine skis have a contribution margin ratio of 20%, while the contribution margin ratio of Nordic skis is only 5%. In addition, the Nordic skis appear to have a low manufacturing margin as a percent of sales compared to the Alpine skis. Either the Nordic skis are being sold for too low a price or the variable manufacturing costs are too high. The Eastern territory has a lower contribution margin ratio than does the Western territory. This is because the Eastern territory sells a higher proportion of the lower-margin Nordic skis than does the Western territory. Management may wish to emphasize sales of Alpine skis until the pricing or cost problems in the Nordic line are resolved.

Problem 17-1

(1)

QuickKey Company
Income Statement
For the Month Ended June 30, 20--

Sales		$1,912,500
Cost of goods sold:		
Cost of goods manufactured	$1,396,800	
Less inventory, June 30 (1,500 × $58.20)	87,300	
Cost of goods sold		1,309,500
Gross profit		$ 603,000
Selling and administrative expenses		393,750
Income from operations		$ 209,250

$58.20 = $1,396,800 ÷ 24,000

(2)

QuickKey Company
Income Statement
For the Month Ended June 30, 20--

Sales		$1,912,500
Variable cost of goods sold:		
Variable cost of goods manufactured	$1,264,800	
Less inventory, June 30 (1,500 × $52.70)	79,050	
Variable cost of goods sold		1,185,750
Manufacturing margin		$ 726,750
Variable selling and administrative expenses		270,000
Contribution margin		$ 456,750
Fixed costs:		
Fixed manufacturing costs	$ 132,000	
Fixed selling and administrative expenses	123,750	255,750
Income from operations		$ 201,000

$52.70 = $1,264,800 ÷ 24,000

(3) The income from operations reported under absorption costing exceeds the income from operations reported under variable costing by $8,250 ($209,250 − $201,000). This $8,250 is due to including $8,250 of fixed manufacturing cost in inventory under absorption costing (1,500 units × $5.50, or 1,500 / 24,000 × $132,000). The $8,250 was thus deferred to a future month under absorption costing, while it was included as an expense of June (part of fixed costs) under variable costing.

Problem 17-2

Ho Company
Contribution Margin Analysis
For the Year Ended December 31, 2000

Increase in the amount of sales attributed to:			
Quantity factor:			
Increase in number of units sold in 2000	1,000		
Planned sales price in 2000	× $18.50	$18,500	
Price factor:			
Increase in unit sales price in 2000	$1.50		
Number of units sold in 2000	× 45,000	67,500	
Net increase in amount of sales			$86,000
Increase in the amount of variable cost of goods sold attributed to:			
Quantity factor:			
Increase in number of units sold in 2000	1,000		
Planned variable cost per unit in 2000	× $8.40	$ 8,400	
Unit cost factor:			
Increase in variable cost per unit in 2000	$0.10		
Number of units sold in 2000	× 45,000	4,500	
Net increase in amount of variable cost of goods sold			12,900
Decrease in the amount of variable selling and administrative expenses attributed to:			
Quantity factor:			
Increase in number of units sold in 2000	1,000		
Planned variable selling and administrative cost per unit in 2000	× $5.60	$ 5,600	
Unit cost factor:			
Decrease in variable selling and administrative cost per unit in 2000	$0.30		
Number of units sold in 2000	× 45,000	13,500	
Net decrease in amount of variable selling and administrative expenses			7,900
Increase in contribution margin			$81,000

CHAPTER 18

Fill In the Blank—Part A

1. budget
2. planning
3. responsibility center
4. control
5. slack
6. goal conflict
7. fiscal year
8. Accounting
9. static
10. relevant activity levels
11. master budget
12. quantity of estimated sales
13. expected unit selling price
14. 164,000
15. production
16. balance sheet budgets
17. cash
18. capital expenditures
19. 84,000
20. $1,500,000

Fill In the Blank—Part B

1. directing
2. feedback
3. tightly
4. budgetary slack
5. goal conflict
6. continuous budgeting
7. zero-based
8. static budget
9. flexible budget
10. computerized
11. sales
12. factory overhead cost
13. cost of goods sold
14. capital expenditures
15. past sales volumes
16. production
17. direct labor cost
18. budgeted income statement
19. $56,000
20. $18,500

Multiple Choice

1. c	6. b
2. a	7. a
3. d	8. b
4. c	9. d
5. c	10. a

True/False

1. F	6. F
2. T	7. T
3. F	8. F
4. T	9. F
5. T	10. T

Exercise 18-1

Texier Inc.
Sales Budget
For the Month of May, 20--

Product and Area	Unit Sales Volume	Unit Selling Price	Total Sales
Product C:			
East area	60,000	$15	$ 900,000
West area	80,000	20	1,600,000
Total	140,000		$2,500,000
Product Q:			
East area	75,000	$ 8	$ 600,000
West area	50,000	10	500,000
Total	125,000		$1,100,000
Total revenue from sales			$3,600,000

Texier Inc.
Production Budget
For the Month of May, 20--

	Units	
	Product C	Product Q
Sales	140,000	125,000
Plus desired inventory, May 31	28,000	25,000
Total	168,000	150,000
Less estimated inventory, May 1	8,000	21,000
Total production	160,000	129,000

Exercise 18-2

Nathalie Inc.
Factory Overhead Cost Budget
For the Month of January, 20--

	30,000	60,000	90,000
Units of product			
Variable cost:			
Indirect factory wages	$ 24,000	$ 48,000	$ 72,000
Indirect materials	13,500	27,000	40,500
Electric power	18,000	36,000	54,000
Total variable cost	$ 55,500	$111,000	$166,500
Fixed cost:			
Supervisory salaries	$ 30,000	$ 30,000	$ 30,000
Depreciation of plant and equipment	18,000	18,000	18,000
Property taxes	12,000	12,000	12,000
Insurance	7,500	7,500	7,500
Electric power	4,500	4,500	4,500
Total fixed cost	$ 72,000	$ 72,000	$ 72,000
Total factory overhead cost	$127,500	$183,000	$238,500

Problem 18-1

Amant Inc.
Cash Budget
For Two Months Ending April 30, 20--

	March	April
Estimated cash receipts from:		
Cash sales	$ 96,000	$ 80,000
Collections of accounts receivable	160,200	124,800
Total cash receipts	$256,200	$204,800
Estimated cash disbursements for:		
Merchandise costs	$130,000	$140,000
Operating expenses	34,000	28,000
Capital expenditures	—	125,000
Property taxes	5,000	—
Total cash disbursements	$169,000	$293,000
Cash increase or (decrease)	$ 87,200	$ (88,200)
Cash balance at beginning of month	24,000	111,200
Cash balance at end of month	$111,200	$ 23,000
Minimum cash balance	50,000	50,000
Excess or (deficiency)	$ 61,200	$ (27,000)

Problem 18-2

(1) Production Budget	Product A	Product B
Sales	168,000	324,000
Plus: desired ending inventory	8,000	36,000
Less: estimated beginning inventory	(12,000)	(24,000)
Total production	164,000	336,000

(2) Direct Materials Purchases Budget

	Material X	Material Y	Material Z	Total
Pounds required for production:				
Product A	98,400		196,800	
Product B	604,800	1,142,400		
Plus desired ending inventory	14,500	8,700	9,800	
Total	717,700	1,151,100	206,600	
Less: estimated beginning inventory	(16,000)	(5,600)	(12,400)	
Total pounds to be purchased	701,700	1,145,500	194,200	
Price per pound	× $0.40	× $0.50	× $0.60	
Total direct materials purchases	$280,680	$ 572,750	$116,520	$969,950

(3) Direct Labor Cost Budget

	Department 1	Department 2	Total
Product A hours	32,800	24,600	
Product B hours	16,800	33,600	
Total hours	49,600	58,200	
Hourly departmental rate	× $14.00	× $18.00	
Total direct labor cost	$694,400	$1,047,600	$1,742,000

CHAPTER 19

Fill In the Blank—Part A

1. standard cost systems
2. principle of exceptions
3. theoretical (or ideal)
4. currently attainable (or normal)
5. quantity
6. purchasing
7. cost variance
8. total manufacturing
9. direct materials quantity variance
10. $700
11. direct labor time variance
12. $1,900
13. controllable
14. $3,000
15. volume variance
16. total factory overhead cost
17. factory overhead cost variance report
18. Direct Materials Quantity Variance
19. cost of goods sold
20. nonfinancial performance

Fill In the Blank—Part B

1. standard cost system
2. engineers
3. theoretical (or ideal) standards
4. currently attainable (or normal)
5. budgetary performance evaluation
6. budget performance
7. unfavorable
8. direct materials price variance
9. unfavorable materials quantity variance
10. purchasing department
11. $320
12. direct labor rate variance
13. $1,100
14. production supervisors
15. flexible
16. controllable variance
17. controllable variance
18. $1,000
19. Direct Materials Price Variance
20. nonfinancial

Multiple Choice

1. a	6. a		
2. c	7. d		
3. b	8. c		
4. d	9. d		
5. b	10. a		

True/False

1. T	6. F		
2. F	7. F		
3. T	8. T		
4. F	9. F		
5. T	10. T		

Exercise 19-1

(1) Price variance:

Actual price	$1.82 per lb.	
Standard price	1.80 per lb.	
Variance—unfavorable	$ .02 per lb. × actual qty., 77,000 lbs.	$1,540

Quantity variance:

Actual quantity	77,000 lbs.	
Standard quantity	75,000 lbs.	
Variance—unfavorable	2,000 lbs. × standard price, $1.80	3,600
Total direct materials cost variance—unfavorable		$5,140

(2) Rate variance:

Actual rate	$19.75 per hr.	
Standard rate	20.00 per hr.	
Variance—favorable	$ (.25) per hr. × actual time, 42,500 hrs.	$(10,625)

Time variance:

Actual time	42,500 hrs..	
Standard time	42,000 hrs.	
Variance—unfavorable	500 hrs. × standard rate, $20.00	10,000
Total direct labor cost variance—favorable		$ (625)

Exercise 19-2

Volume variance:

100% of normal capacity	40,000 hours	
Standard for amount produced	30,000 hours	
Productive capacity not used	10,000 hours	
Standard fixed factory overhead rate	× $3	
Variance—unfavorable		$30,000

Controllable variance:

Actual variable factory overhead	$153,500	
Budgeted variable factory overhead for 30,000 hours	150,000	
Variance—unfavorable		3,500
Total factory overhead cost variance—unfavorable		$33,500

Exercise 19-3

Nathalie Inc.
Budget Performance Report—Factory Overhead Cost
For Month Ended January 31, 20--

	Budget	Actual	Unfavorable	Favorable
Variable cost:				
Indirect factory wages	$ 48,000	$ 50,500	$2,500	
Indirect materials	27,000	27,600	600	
Electric power	36,000	35,000		$1,000
Total variable cost	$111,000	$113,100		
Fixed cost:				
Supervisory salaries	$ 30,000	$ 30,000		
Depr. of plant and equipment	18,000	18,000		
Property taxes	12,000	12,000		
Insurance	7,500	7,500		
Electric power	4,500	4,500		
Total fixed cost	72,000	72,000		
Total factory overhead cost	$183,000	$185,100	$3,100	$1,000

Exercise 19-4

(1)
```
      30  employees
×     40  hours per week
   1,200  total hours worked
×    $16  labor rate per hour
 $19,200  IRS labor cost
```

(2) Flexible budget:

No. of traditional paper returns processed .... 1,300 × 45 min. = 58,500 min.
No. of electronic returns processed .... 225 × 8 min. = 1,800 min.
                                                                   60,300 min.

60,300 / 60 = 1,005 hours flexible budget

(3) Time variance:

Actual time .... 1,005 hours
Standard time .... 1,200 hours
    Variance—favorable .... (195) hours × $16 rate = $(3,120)

Problem 19-1

(1)   Direct Materials Cost Variances

		Variance
Price variance:		
Actual price	$6.20 per lb.	
Standard price	6.00 per lb.	
Variance	$ .20 per lb. × actual qty., 250,000 lbs.	$50,000 U
Quantity variance:		
Actual quantity	250,000 lbs.	
Standard quantity	255,000 lbs.	
Variance	(5,000) lbs. × standard price, $6	30,000 F
Total direct materials cost variance		$20,000 U

(2)   Direct Labor Cost Variances

		Variance
Rate variance:		
Actual rate	$14.60 per hr.	
Standard rate	15.00 per hr.	
Variance	$ (.40) per hr. × actual time, 77,400 hrs.	$30,960 F
Time variance:		
Actual time	77,400 hrs.	
Standard time	76,500 hrs.	
Variance	900 hrs. × standard rate, $15	13,500 U
Total direct labor cost variance		$17,460 F

(3)

<u>Factory Overhead Cost Variances</u>

Variance

Controllable variance:

Actual variable factory overhead cost incurred	$160,000	
Budgeted variable factory overhead for actual product produced	153,000	
Variance		$ 7,000 U

Volume variance:

Budgeted hours at 100% of normal capacity	90,000 hrs.	
Standard hours for amount produced	76,500 hrs.	
Productive capacity not used	13,500 hrs.	
Standard fixed factory overhead cost rate	× $1.50	
Variance		20,250 U
Total factory overhead cost variance		$27,250 U

Problem 19-2

Piazza Company, Inc.
Income Statement
For the Month Ended January 31, 20--

Sales		$995,000
Cost of goods sold—at standard		812,000
Gross profit—at standard		$183,000

	Favorable	Unfavorable		
Less variances from standard cost:				
Direct materials price		$ 500		
Direct materials quantity		1,500		
Direct labor rate		1,200		
Direct labor time	$3,000			
Factory overhead controllable	4,000			
Factory overhead volume		10,000	6,200	
Gross profit			$176,800	
Operating expenses:				
Selling expenses		$68,000		
Administrative expenses		42,000	110,000	
Income before income tax			$ 66,800	

CHAPTER 20

Fill In the Blank—Part A

1. centralized
2. responsibility centers
3. responsibility accounting
4. cost center
5. more
6. revenues
7. controllable
8. service department charges
9. activity base
10. $48,000
11. $53,000
12. investment center
13. rate of return on investment (or on assets)
14. profit margin
15. 8%
16. 3.125
17. 25%
18. residual income
19. market price
20. negotiated price

Fill In the Blank—Part B

1. decentralization
2. responsibility center
3. investment centers
4. costs
5. more
6. profit center
7. controllable
8. service department charges
9. indirect
10. $38,400
11. $68,000
12. residual income
13. invested assets
14. investment turnover
15. 8%
16. 2.5
17. 20%
18. nonfinancial performance measures
19. transfer price
20. market price

Multiple Choice   **True/False**

1. a	**6.** b	**1.** T	**6.** T
2. b	**7.** c	**2.** T	**7.** F
3. c	**8.** a	**3.** F	**8.** F
4. d	**9.** d	**4.** F	**9.** T
5. d	**10.** c	**5.** T	**10.** F

Exercise 20-1

(1) **(a)** $280,000   **(c)** $520,000
    (b) $120,000   **(d)** $135,000

(2) Division M: 16% ($120,000 / $750,000)
    Division N: 22% ($110,000 / $500,000)

(3) Division M

(4) Division N

Exercise 20-2

(1) Division M:

Income from operations	$120,000
Minimum income ($750,000 × 12%)	90,000
Residual income	$ 30,000

   Division N:

Income from operations	$110,000
Minimum income ($500,000 × 12%)	60,000
Residual income	$ 50,000

(2) Division N

Exercise 20-3

(a) 1.6
(b) 12.5%
(c) 18.9%
(d) 18%
(e) 1.5

Problem 20-1

Budget Performance Report—Supervisor, Department F, Plant 7
For Month Ended July 31, 20--

	Budget	Actual	Over	Under
Factory wages	$ 65,000	$ 73,600	$8,600	
Materials	39,500	37,700		$1,800
Supervisory salaries	15,000	15,000		
Power and light	8,900	9,600	700	
Depr. of plant and equipment	7,500	7,500		
Maintenance	4,300	3,900		400
Insurance and property taxes	2,000	2,000		
	$142,200	$149,300	$9,300	$2,200

Problem 20-2

Firefly Co.
Income Statement—Divisions J and K
For the Year Ended May 31, 20--

	Division J	Division K	Total
Net sales	$280,000	$420,000	$700,000
Cost of goods sold	122,500	227,500	350,000
Gross profit	$157,500	$192,500	$350,000
Operating expenses	48,000	72,000	120,000
Income from operations before service department charges	$109,500	$120,500	$230,000
Less service department charges:			
Payroll accounting	$ 24,000	$ 36,000	$ 60,000
Purchasing	48,400	39,600	88,000
Brochure advertising	31,250	18,750	50,000
Total service department charges	$103,650	$ 94,350	$198,000
Income from operations	$ 5,850	$ 26,150	$ 32,000

Supporting Schedules:

	Number of Payroll Checks	Number of Requisitions	Number of Brochure Pages
Division J	400	2,200	500
Division K	600	1,800	300
Total	1,000	4,000	800
Relative percentages:			
Division J	40.00%	55.00%	62.50%
Division K	60.00%	45.00%	37.50%
Service department costs	$60,000	$88,000	$50,000
Percentages multiplied by service department costs:			
Division J	24,000	48,400	31,250
Division K	36,000	39,600	18,750

Problem 20-3

(1) (a) no effect
    (b) no effect

(2) (a) increase by $30,000
    (b) increase by $50,000

(3) (a) increase by $100,000
    (b) decrease by $20,000

CHAPTER 21

Fill In the Blank—Part A

1. differential revenue
2. differential cost
3. sunk cost
4. income tax differential
5. $68,000
6. $5
7. opportunity cost
8. further processing
9. variable
10. variable costs
11. demand-based
12. competition-based
13. total costs
14. total fixed costs
15. 10%
16. 65%
17. 83.3%
18. activity-based costing
19. production bottle-neck (or constraint)
20. theory of constraints

Fill In the Blank—Part B

1. differential analysis
2. sunk costs
3. differential income (or loss)
4. differential revenues
5. $79,000
6. capacity
7. opportunity cost
8. $.30
9. Robinson-Patman Act
10. total cost
11. product cost
12. variable cost
13. total cost
14. total cost
15. total manufacturing costs
16. 12.5%
17. 80%
18. 50%
19. target cost concept
20. production bottle-neck (or constraint)

Multiple Choice

1. c
2. a
3. b
4. b
5. d
6. d
7. c
8. b
9. a
10. c

True/False

1. T
2. F
3. F
4. F
5. F
6. T
7. T
8. T
9. T
10. F

Exercise 21-1

Differential revenue from alternatives:		
Revenue from lease	$20,000	
Revenue from sale	18,000	
Differential revenue from lease		$2,000
Differential cost of alternatives:		
License expenses during lease	$ 1,100	
Repainting expense on sale	900	
Differential cost of leasing		200
Net differential income (loss) from lease alternative		$1,800

Exercise 21-2

Purchase price of blades		$14.00
Differential cost to manufacture blades:		
Direct materials	$6.75	
Direct labor	5.10	
Variable factory overhead	.80	12.65
Cost savings (increase) from manufacturing blades		$ 1.35

Exercise 21-3

Differential revenue from sales of rocking chairs:		
Revenue from sales		$350,000
Differential cost of sales of rocking chairs:		
Variable cost of goods sold	$180,000	
Variable operating expenses	75,000	255,000
Differential income (loss) from sales of rocking chairs		$ 95,000

The rocking chairs section probably should be continued.

Exercise 21-4

Annual variable costs—present machine	$ 65,000	
Annual variable costs—new machine	30,000	
Annual differential decrease (increase) in variable costs	$ 35,000	
Number of years applicable	× 7	
Total differential decrease (increase) in variable costs	$245,000	
Proceeds from sale of present machine	83,000	$328,000
Cost of new machine		370,000
Net differential decrease (increase) in cost, seven-year total		$(42,000)
Annual net differential decrease (increase) in cost—new machine		$ (6,000)

Problem 21-1

(1) $60,000 ($500,000 × 12%)

(2) **(a)** Total costs:

Variable ($5 × 50,000 units)	$250,000
Fixed ($35,000 + $15,000)	50,000
Total	$300,000

Cost amount per unit: $300,000 / 50,000 units = $6

(b) Markup Percentage = Desired Profit / Total Costs
Markup Percentage = $60,000 / $300,000
Markup Percentage = 20%

(c)

Cost amount per unit	$6.00
Markup ($6 × 20%)	1.20
Selling price	$7.20

Problem 21-2

(1) Total manufacturing costs:

Variable ($4 × 50,000 units)	$200,000
Fixed factory overhead	35,000
Total	$235,000

Cost amount per unit: $235,000 / 50,000 units = $4.70

(2) Markup Percentage = (Desired Profit + Total Selling and Administrative Expenses) / Total Manufacturing Costs
Markup Percentage = [$60,000 + $15,000 + ($1 × 50,000 units)] / $235,000
Markup Percentage = $125,000 / $235,000
Markup Percentage = 53.2%

(3)

Cost amount per unit	$4.70
Markup ($4.70 × 53.2%)	2.50
Selling price	$7.20

Problem 21-3

(1) Total variable costs: $5 × 50,000 units = $250,000
Cost amount per unit: $250,000 / 50,000 units = $5

(2) Markup Percentage = Desired Profit + Total Fixed Costs / Total Variable Costs
Markup Percentage = ($60,000 + $35,000 + $15,000) / $250,000
Markup Percentage = $110,000 / $250,000
Markup Percentage = 44%

(3) Cost amount per unit $5.00
Markup ($5 × 44%) .... _2.20_
Selling price .... _$7.20_

Problem 21-4

First, determine the contribution margin per bottleneck hour for each product.

	Product D	Product E	Product F
Sales price per unit	$750	$600	$400
Variable cost per unit	300	350	200
Contribution margin per unit	$450	$250	$200
Furnace hours per unit	÷ 15	÷ 10	÷ 8
Contribution margin per furnace hour (CM ÷ furnace hours)	$ 30	$ 25	$ 25

Product D is more profitable in per furnace hour terms than either Products E or F. Products E and F would need to increase prices enough to make their contribution margin per furnace hour equal to $30.

Product E: $(X - \$350) / 10$ furnace hours = $30
$X - \$350 = \$300$
$X = \$650$

Product F: $(X - \$200) / 8$ furnace hours = $30
$X - \$200 = \$240$
$X = \$440$

CHAPTER 22

Fill In the Blank—Part A

1. capital investment analysis (or capital budgeting)
2. internal rate of return
3. short
4. 25%   [$53,500 / ($400,000 + $28,000 / 2)]
5. average rate of return
6. cash payback
7. 6 years   [$300,000 / ($65,000 − $15,000)]
8. cash payback
9. annuity
10. net present value (or discounted cash flow)
11. $9,550   [($50,000 × 3.791) − $180,000]
12. index
13. net present value (or discounted cash flow)
14. annual net cash flows
15. highest
16. uncertainty
17. same
18. strategic
19. qualitative
20. minimum

Fill In the Blank—Part B

1. present values
2. cash payback
3. time value
4. average rate of return (or accounting rate of return)
5. 25%   [($270,000 ÷ 3) / ($680,000 + $40,000) ÷ 2]
6. net cash flow
7. cash payback period
8. timing
9. present value of an annuity
10. net present value
11. $12,060   [($30,000 × .893) + ($30,000 × .797) + ($30,000 × .712)] − $60,000
12. 1.44   ($72,000 / $50,000)
13. internal rate of return (or time-adjusted rate of return)
14. $5,200   [($10,000 × 3.170) − $26,500]
15. 4.975   ($79,600 / $16,000)
16. internal rate of return
17. leasing
18. inflation
19. rationing
20. strategic investments

Multiple Choice

1. a	**6.** a
2. d	**7.** c
3. c	**8.** d
4. b	**9.** c
5. b	**10.** d

True/False

1. T	**6.** F
2. T	**7.** T
3. F	**8.** T
4. F	**9.** T
5. F	**10.** F

Exercise 22-1

(1) $48,000 / $310,000 = 15.48%

(2) $620,000 / $200,000 = 3.1 years

(3) Yes. The proposal meets the minimum rate of return desired.

(4) No. The proposal does not meet the minimum cash payback period desired.

Exercise 22-2

Proposal 1: $250,000 / $60,000 = 4.17 years

Proposal 2:

Year	Net Cash Flow	Cumulative Net Cash Flow
1	$100,000	$100,000
2	80,000	180,000
3	70,000	250,000
4	45,000	295,000
5	45,000	340,000
6	20,000	360,000

The cumulative net cash flow at the end of three years equals the amount of the investment, $250,000, so the payback period is three years.

Exercise 22-3

Proposal 1: The factor for the present value of an annuity for 6 years at 10%: 4.355

$60,000 × 4.355	$261,300
Less amount invested	250,000
Net present value	$ 11,300

Proposal 2:

Year	Present Value of 1 at 10%	Net Cash Flow	Present Value of Net Cash Flow
1	0.909	$100,000	$ 90,900
2	0.826	80,000	66,080
3	0.751	70,000	52,570
4	0.683	45,000	30,735
5	0.621	45,000	27,945
6	0.564	20,000	11,280
Total		$360,000	$279,510
Amount to be invested in equipment			250,000
Excess of present value over amount to be invested			$ 29,510

Exercise 22-4

(1) Present Value Factor for an Annuity of $1 = Amount to be Invested / Annual Net Cash Flow
Present Value Factor for an Annuity of $1 = $358,900 / $120,000
Present Value Factor for an Annuity of $1 = 2.991

(2) 20%

Problem 22-1

(1)

Year	Present Value of 1 at 12%	Net Cash Flow	Present Value of Net Cash Flow
1	0.893	$ 80,000	$ 71,440
2	0.797	60,000	47,820
3	0.712	60,000	42,720
4	0.636	60,000	38,160
5	0.567	60,000	34,020
Total		$320,000	$234,160

Amount to be invested in equipment 180,000

Excess of present value over amount to be invested .... $ 54,160

(2) 1.30 ($234,160 / $180,000)

(3) yes

Problem 22-2

(1) Project 1:

Year	Present Value of 1 at 10%	Net Cash Flow	Present Value of Net Cash Flow
1	0.909	$ 55,000	$ 49,995
2	0.826	50,000	41,300
3	0.751	45,000	33,795
4	0.683	40,000	27,320
5	0.621	40,000	24,840
6	0.564	30,000	16,920
7	0.513	15,000	7,695
Total		$275,000	$201,865

Amount to be invested 180,000

Net present value .... $ 21,865

Project 2:

Year	Present Value of 1 at 10%	Net Cash Flow	Present Value of Net Cash Flow
1	0.909	$ 55,000	$ 49,995
2	0.826	55,000	45,430
3	0.751	55,000	41,305
4	0.683	55,000	37,565
5	0.621	55,000	34,155
Total		$275,000	$208,450

Amount to be invested 180,000

Net present value .... $ 28,450

(2) Project 1:

Year	Present Value of 1 at 10%	Net Cash Flow	Present Value of Net Cash Flow
1	0.909	$ 55,000	$ 49,995
2	0.826	50,000	41,300
3	0.751	45,000	33,795
4	0.683	40,000	27,320
5	0.621	40,000	24,840
5 Res. value	0.621	60,000	37,260
Total		$290,000	$214,510

Amount to be invested 180,000

Net present value .... $ 34,510

(3) Using a 5-year analysis, Project 1's net present value, $34,510, is greater than Project 2's, $28,450; thus Project 1 is more attractive.

CHAPTER 23

Fill In the Blank—Part A

1. product costing
2. total budgeted factory overhead cost, total budgeted plantwide allocation base
3. $288
   (24 machine hours × $12 per machine hour)
4. production department.
5. $60 per direct labor hour
   ($420,000 ÷ 7,000 direct labor hours)
6. $480   ($32 × 15 hours)
7. distortion
8. equal to
9. differences
10. ratio
11. pools
12. $40 per unit   ($400 × 12 setups) / (12 setups × 10 units), or $400 / 10 units
13. $30 per purchase order
    ($360,000 ÷ 12,000 purchase orders)
14. complex
15. number of inspections
16. period, product
17. sales
18. $6,850   ($36 × 150) + ($145 × 10)
19. $14,450   ($36 × 200) + ($145 × 50)
20. patient

Fill In the Blank—B

1. activity-based costing
2. simplicity
3. different
4. activity base
5. equal to
6. multiple production department rate
7. single plantwide rate
8. engineering change order
9. setup
10. allocation base
11. no
12. no
13. yes
14. no
15. strategies
16. $425
17. $5,100
18. $28
19. can
20. number of images

Multiple Choice

1. a		6. b	
2. a		7. a	
3. c		8. a	
4. b		9. c*	
5. d		10. b**	

True/False

1. T		6. F	
2. F		7. F	
3. F		8. T	
4. T		9. T	
5. F		10. F	

* ($290,000 ÷ 2,900 railcars)
** ($100 per railcar × 60 railcars) + ($17.60 per mile × 550 miles)

Exercise 23-1

(1) Total factory overhead is $1,040,000. The selling and administrative expenses are not *factory* overhead and should not be included in determining the plantwide rate.

Total direct labor hours:

	Budgeted Production Volume	×	Direct Labor Hours per Unit	=	Direct Labor Hours
Casual	450,000		0.1		45,000
Work	200,000		0.2		40,000
Dress	150,000		0.3		45,000
	800,000				130,000

Single plantwide factory overhead rate: $\dfrac{\$1,040,000}{130,000 \text{ direct labor hours}}$ = $8 per direct labor hour

(2)

	Direct Labor Hours	×	Single Plantwide Factory Overhead Rate per Direct Labor Hour	=	Factory Overhead	Factory Overhead per Unit (Factory Overhead ÷ Budgeted Production Volume)
Casual	45,000		$8		$ 360,000	÷ 450,000 units = $0.80
Work	40,000		8		320,000	÷ 200,000 units = 1.60
Dress	45,000		8		360,000	÷ 150,000 units = 2.40
Total	130,000				$1,040,000	

Exercise 23-2

(1) Production department factory overhead rates:

	Press Department	Cure Department
Total factory overhead	$600,000	$240,000
Machine hours	÷ 8,000 mh	÷ 24,000 mh
Departmental overhead rate	$ 75/mh	$ 10/mh

(2)

	Auto Brake	Truck Brake	Bus Brake
Machine hours per unit—Press Dept.	0.3	0.5	1
Press Dept. factory overhead rate	× $75/mh	× $75/mh	× $75/mh
Press Dept. factory overhead	$22.50	$37.50	$ 75.00
Machine hours per unit—Cure Dept.	2.25	2.5	3
Cure Dept. factory overhead rate	× $10/mh	× $10/mh	× $10/mh
Cure Dept. factory overhead	22.50	25.00	30.00
Total factory overhead per set	$45.00	$62.50	$105.00

Exercise 23-3

(1)

	Purchasing	Inspecting	Materials Handling	Product Engineering
Activity cost pool	$225,000	$140,000	$70,000	$165,000
Activity base	÷ 10,000 POs	÷ 7,000 insp.	÷35,000 moves	÷ 1,000 ECOs
Activity rate	$ 22.50/PO	$ 20/insp.	$ 2/move	$ 165/ECO

(2) Laser Printer:

	Activity-Base Usage	×	Activity Rate	=	Activity Cost
Purchasing	4,000 purch. orders		$22.50/purch. order		$ 90,000
Inspecting	5,500 inspections		$20/inspection		110,000
Materials handling	20,000 moves		$2/move		40,000
Product development	800 ECOs		$165/ECO		132,000
Total activity cost					$372,000
Unit volume					÷ 4,000
Activity cost per unit					$ 93

Ink Jet printer:

	Activity-Base Usage	×	Activity Rate	=	Activity Cost
Purchasing	6,000 purch. orders		$22.50/purch. order		$135,000
Inspecting	1,500 inspections		$20/inspection		30,000
Materials handling	15,000 moves		$2/move		30,000
Product development	200 ECOs		$165/ECO		33,000
Total activity cost					$228,000
Unit volume					÷ 4,000
Activity cost per unit					$ 57

Problem 23-1

(1) Production department rates:

	Cutting Department	Assembly Department
Factory overhead	$1,200,000	$600,000
Direct labor hours	÷ 10,000 dlh	÷ 10,000 dlh
Production department rate	$ 120/dlh	$ 60/dlh

(2) Suitcase:

	Direct Labor Hours	×	Production Department Rate	=	Factory Overhead
Cutting	8,000		$120/dlh		$ 960,000
Assembly	2,000		$60/dlh		120,000
Total factory overhead					$1,080,000
Number of units					÷ 10,000
Factory overhead per unit					$ 108

Garment Bag:

	Direct Labor Hours	×	Production Department Rate	=	Factory Overhead
Cutting	2,000		$120/dlh		$240,000
Assembly	8,000		$60/dlh		480,000
Total factory overhead					$720,000
Number of units					÷ 10,000
Factory overhead per unit					$ 72

(3) Activity-based rates:

	Inspecting	Setup	Cutting	Assembly
Activity cost pool	$600,000	$200,000	$800,000	$200,000
Activity base	÷ 4,000 insp.	÷ 800 setups	÷ 10,000 dlh	÷ 10,000 dlh
Activity rate	$ 150/insp.	$ 250/setup	$ 80/dlh	$ 20/dlh

(4) Suitcase:

	Activity-Base Usage	×	Activity Rate	=	Activity Cost
Inspecting	1,000 inspections		$150/inspection		$150,000
Setup	200 setups		$250/setup		50,000
Cutting	8,000 dlh		$80/dlh		640,000
Assembly	2,000 dlh		$20/dlh		40,000
Total					$880,000
Number of units					÷ 10,000
Activity cost per unit					$ 88

Garment Bag:

	Activity-Base Usage	×	Activity Rate	=	Activity Cost
Inspecting	3,000 inspections		$150/inspection		$450,000
Setup	600 setups		$250/setup		150,000
Cutting	2,000 dlh		$80/dlh		160,000
Assembly	8,000 dlh		$20/dlh		160,000
Total					$920,000
Number of units					÷ 10,000
Activity cost per unit					$ 92

(5) The activity-based overhead assignment reveals that garment bags are more costly than suitcases on a per unit basis. The multiple production department rate method does not show this because the method assumes that all factory overhead is proportional to direct labor hours. Since each product consumes the same total direct labor hours, the factory overhead assignment is nearly equal. The activity-based method separately accounts for the inspecting and setup activity costs. Garment bags have more inspecting and setup activities than do suitcases Thus, garment bags are shown to have higher activity costs per unit than do suitcases.

Problem 23-2

(1)

	1-800 Support	Return Processing	Order Processing
Activity cost	$5,400,000	$7,200,000	$9,000,000
Activity base	÷ 50,000 calls	÷ 12,000 returns	÷ 45,000 orders
Activity rate	$ 108/call	$ 600/return	$ 200/order

(2)

	Integrated Accounting		Human Resource		Project Management	
Number of customer 1-800 calls	20,000		20,000		10,000	
Activity rate per call	× $108		× $108		× $108	
1-800 support cost		$2,160,000		$2,160,000		$1,080,000
Number of returns	2,000		5,000		5,000	
Activity rate per return	× $600		× $600		× $600	
Product return processing cost		1,200,000		3,000,000		3,000,000
Number of sales orders	20,000		15,000		10,000	
Activity rate per order	× $200		× $200		× $200	
Sales order processing cost		4,000,000		3,000,000		2,000,000
Total nonmanufacturing activity costs		$7,360,000		$8,160,000		$6,080,000

(3)

	Integrated Accounting	Human Resource	Project Management
Revenues	$25,000,000	$20,000,000	$ 5,000,000
Less cost of goods sold	2,500,000	2,000,000	500,000
Gross profit	$22,500,000	$18,000,000	$ 4,500,000
Less:			
1-800 support	$ 2,160,000	$ 2,160,000	$ 1,080,000
Return processing	1,200,000	3,000,000	3,000,000
Sales order processing	4,000,000	3,000,000	2,000,000
Total activity cost	$ 7,360,000	$ 8,160,000	$ 6,080,000
Operating income	$15,140,000	$ 9,840,000	$(1,580,000)

(4) Project management software is unprofitable, while the other two products have healthy margins. This is because the project management software has excessive 1-800 support calls, product returns (approximately 50% of unit volume!), and sales order activities relative to its volume. For example, the project management software averages one 1-800 call per unit sold, sells only one unit per order, and has half of the units returned. The company's options include the following:

a. Drop project management software. This does not necessarily mean that all the costs can be avoided. The costs will only go away if the reduced activity translates into lower expenditures. Thus, the company should evaluate the contribution margin of this product before making this decision.

b. Increase the price on the project software. Charge customers a higher price to compensate for the higher activities required to serve this software. However, the customers may not accept the price increase required to make this a profitable product.

c. Redesign the instructions to the software to reduce the amount of 1-800 call support for this product. Also, improve the product to reduce the high percentage of returns and 1-800 support calls. Apparently this software is having trouble in the field.

d. Price 1-800 customer support as a separate service. In other words, unbundle the pricing of goods from the support services.

e. Improve the efficiency of order processing. Each order costs $200 to process. For a $500 product, this seems excessive. There should be some opportunity for some process savings in this area.

f. Move the support and ordering to the Internet.

CHAPTER 24

Fill In the Blank—Part A

1. just-in-time manufacturing
2. reduce
3. lead time
4. value-added lead time
5. lead time
6. 16 minutes
7. 796 minutes
   (49 units × 16 minutes) + 12 minutes
8. setup
9. process-oriented layout
10. employee involvement
11. kanban
12. supplier partnering
13. $105
    ($175,000 ÷ 250 hours) × (9 min. ÷ 60 min.)
14. $358,333 [(250 hours × 60 min.) ÷ 9 min.] × ($105 + $110)
15. directly assigned
16. nonfinancial
17. $500 per hour
18. external failure
19. Pareto chart
20. value-added

Fill In the Blank—B

1. just-in-time manufacturing
2. make to stock
3. pull
4. product-oriented
5. nonvalue-added lead time
6. 28 minutes
7. 659 minutes
   (23 units × 28 minutes) + 15 minutes
8. Pareto chart
9. materials, work in process
10. cross-trained
11. electronic data interchange
12. $450
    ($360,000 ÷ 240 hours) × (18 min. ÷ 60 min.)
13. $420,000 [(240 hours × 60 min.) ÷ 18 min.] × ($450 + $75)
14. $70
15. nonfinancial
16. internal failure
17. prevention
18. nonvalue-added
19. internal, external
20. cost of quality report

Multiple Choice

1. b	6. c*
2. c	7. b**
3. d	8. c
4. a	9. a
5. a	10. b***

True/False

1. F	6. F
2. F	7. T
3. T	8. F
4. F	9. T
5. T	10. F

* {[$175 × (18 min. / 60 min.)] + $48} × 300 units
** (15 units × $100.50)
*** ($60,000 + $90,000) / $400,000

Exercise 24-1

	Traditional	JIT
Process Step 1	3	3
Process Step 2	7	7
Process Step 3	12	12
Process Step 4	5	5
Total value-added time	27	27
Number of moves	5	5
Minutes per move	× 15	× 5
Move time	75	25
Units waiting their turn (Batch size − 1)	39	2
Total processing minutes per unit	× 27	× 27
Within-batch wait time	1,053	54

	Traditional		JIT	
	Time	Percent of Total Lead Time	Time	Percent of Total Lead Time
Total nonvalue-added time (move time + within-batch wait time)	1,128	97.7%	79	74 5%
Value-added process time per unit	27	2.3%	27	25.5%
Total lead time per unit	1,155		106	

Exercise 24-2

(1) Cell conversion cost per hour:

$$\frac{\$1,845,000}{2,050 \text{ hours}} = \$900 \text{ per hour}$$

(2) Cell conversion cost per unit:

$$\frac{10 \text{ minutes}}{60 \text{ minutes}} \times \$900 \text{ per hour} = \$150 \text{ per unit}$$

(3) (a)

Raw and In Process Inventory	138,375	
Accounts Payable		138,375
(1,025 units × $135)		

(b)

Raw and In Process Inventory	153,750	
Conversion Cost		153,750
(1,025 units × $150)		

(c)

Finished Goods	292,125	
Raw and In Process Inventory		292,125
[1,025 units × ($135 + $150)]		

(d)

Accounts Receivable	480,000	
Sales		480,000
Cost of Goods Sold (1,000 × $285)	285,000	
Finished Goods		285,000

Exercise 24-3

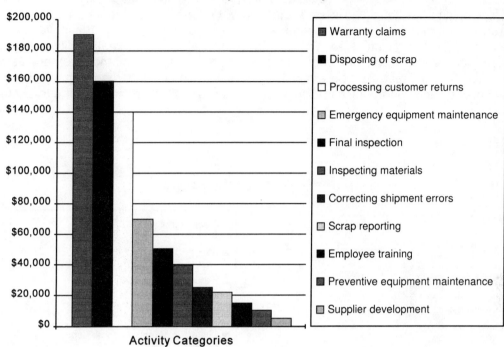

Pareto Chart of Quality Costs—Veracity Instruments

Legend:
- Warranty claims
- Disposing of scrap
- Processing customer returns
- Emergency equipment maintenance
- Final inspection
- Inspecting materials
- Correcting shipment errors
- Scrap reporting
- Employee training
- Preventive equipment maintenance
- Supplier development

X-axis: Activity Categories

Problem 24-1

(1) Value-added time:

Hand soldering of PC board	12 minutes
Device final assembly	18 minutes
Time to inspect one unit	4 minutes
Pack and label	4 minutes
Total	38 minutes

Nonvalue-added time:

Wait time:

Within-batch wait time—PC board soldering (79 × 12 min.)	948 minutes	
Within-batch wait time—Final assembly (79 × 18 min.)	1,422 minutes	
Within-batch wait time—Testing (79 × 4 min.)	316 minutes	
Within-batch wait time—Shipping (79 × 4 min.)	316 minutes	
Test setup	45 minutes	
Total wait time		3,047 minutes

Move time:

Move from PC board assembly to final assembly	10 minutes	
Move from final assembly to testing	30 minutes	
Total move time		40 minutes

Machine breakdown time:

Average breakdown and maintenance time (10% × 80 × 10 min.)	80 minutes	
Total breakdown wait time		80 minutes

Total nonvalue-added time		3,167 minutes

Ratio of nonvalue-added time to total lead time: 3,167 ÷ 3,205 = 98.81%

(2) The existing process is very wasteful. The company could improve the process by changing the layout from a process orientation to a product orientation. Each storage device type could be formed into a production cell. Each cell would have PC card assembly, final assembly, and shipping next to each other. In this way, the batch sizes could be reduced significantly. Workers could practice one-at-a-time processing and merely pass a single completed assembly through the cell. As a result, the move time and within-batch wait time would be eliminated. The company could also initiate total quality principles. Moving toward zero defects would allow the company to reduce testing activities (and time), and as a result the setup time for the test area might be eliminated or reduced. In addition, the company should use more preventive maintenance on the testing machines in order to reduce the amount of unexpected machine downtime.

Problem 24-2

(1)

Pareto Chart of Quality Cost Activity

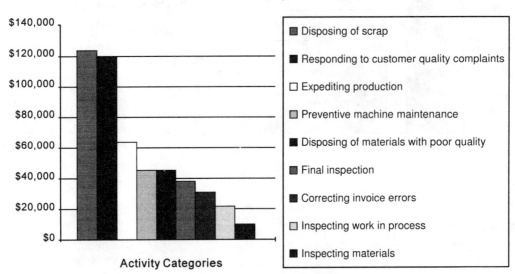

(2) The following quality cost classifications were used in developing the cost of quality report:

Preventive machine maintenance	$45,000	Prevention
Disposing of scrap	125,000	Internal failure
Correcting invoice errors	30,000	External failure
Final inspection	38,000	Appraisal
Expediting production	65,000	Internal failure
Disposing of materials with poor quality	45,000	Internal failure
Responding to customer quality complaints	120,000	External failure
Inspecting work in process	22,000	Appraisal
Producing product	200,000	Not a cost of quality
Inspecting materials	10,000	Appraisal
Total	$700,000	

Kokimo Company
Cost of Quality

	Cost Summary	
Quality Cost Classification	Quality Cost	Percent of Total Quality Cost
Prevention	$ 45,000	9%
Appraisal	70,000	14
Internal failure	235,000	47
External failure	150 000	30
Total	$500,000	100%

(3) The following analysis treats the prevention and appraisal costs as value-added and the internal and external failure costs as nonvalue-added:

Category	Amount	Percent
Value-added	$115,000	23%
Nonvalue-added	385,000	77
Total	$500,000	100%

(4) The company has only 23% of its total costs as value-added. Internal failure costs are 47% and external failure costs are 30% of total quality costs. Prevention activities are only 9% of the total quality cost effort. Kokimo should shift much more of its attention toward prevention and appraisal activities in order to eliminate the internal and external failure costs before they occur. There is significant room for improvement.

STATEMENT OF CASH FLOWS

Fill In the Blank—Part A

1. statement of cash flows
2. direct indirect
3. operating
4. investing
5. investing
6. financing
7. investing
8. increased
9. decreased
10. decreased
11. $34,250
12. $102,000
13. $195,000
14. $60,000
15. $49,500
16. $1,040,000
17. $330,000
18. financing
19. $60,000
20. cash flow per share

Fill In the Blank—Part B

1. indirect
2. operating
3. direct
4. financing
5. financing
6. operating
7. financing
8. investing
9. noncash
10. deducted from
11. added to
12. $330,000
13. $746,250
14. $3,125,000
15. $46,000
16. $20,000
17. retained earnings
18. $51,000
19. operating
20. free cash flow

Multiple Choice

1. b
2. b
3. c
4. d
5. d
6. c
7. b
8. a
9. a
10. c

True/False

1. T
2. T
3. T
4. F
5. F
6. T
7. T
8. T
9. F
10. T

Exercise 1

Item	Cash Flows From — Operating Activities	Cash Flows From — Investing Activities	Cash Flows From — Financing Activities	Schedule of Noncash Investing and Financing Activities
1. Decrease in prepaid expenses	✔			
2. Retirement of bonds			✔	
3. Proceeds from sale of investments		✔		
4. Increase in inventories	✔			
5. Issuance of common stock			✔	
6. Purchase of equipment		✔		

		Cash Flows From			Schedule of Noncash Investing and Financing Activities
	Item	Operating Activities	Investing Activities	Financing Activities	
7.	Cash dividends paid			✔	
8.	Acquisition of building in exchange for bonds				✔
9.	Amortization of patents	✔			
10.	Amortization of discount on bonds payable	✔			

Exercise 2

Cash flows from operating activities:

Net income, per income statement		$150,000
Add: Depreciation	$45,000	
Decrease in prepaid expenses	2,625	
Increase in accounts payable	17,000	64,625
		$214,625
Deduct: Increase in trade receivables	$10,000	
Increase in inventories	15,625	
Decrease in salaries payable	3,000	28,625
Net cash flow from operating activities		$186,000

Exercise 3

Cash flows from operating activities:

Cash received from customers		$520,000
Deduct: Cash payments for merchandise	$128,625	
Cash payments for operating expenses	160,375	
Cash payments for income tax	45,000	334,000
Net cash flow from operating activities		$186,000

Supporting calculations:

Sales (reported on income statement)	$530,000
Less increase in trade receivables	(10,000)
Cash received from customers	$520,000
Cost of merchandise sold	$130,000
Plus increase in inventories	15,625
Less increase in accounts payable	(17,000)
Cash payments for merchandise	$128,625
Operating expenses (other than depreciation)	$160,000
Less decrease in prepaid expenses	(2,625)
Plus decrease in salaries payable	3,000
Cash payments for operating expenses	$160,375

Problem 1

Stellar Inc.
Statement of Cash Flows
For Year Ended December 31, 2001

Cash flows from operating activities:		
Net income, per income statement		$114,000
Add: Depreciation	$48,000	
Decrease in inventories	6,000	
Decrease in prepaid expenses	2,400	
Increase in accounts payable	7,200	63,600
		$177,600
Deduct: Increase in trade receivables	$12,000	
Gain on sale of land	18,000	30,000
Net cash flow from operating activities		$147,600
Cash flows from investing activities:		
Cash received from land sold	$ 54,000	
Less cash paid for purchase of equipment	96,000	
Net cash flow used for investing activities		(42,000)
Cash flows from financing activities:		
Cash used to retire bonds payable	$ 60,000	
Cash paid for dividends	27,600*	
Net cash flow used for financing activities		(87,600)
Increase in cash		$ 18,000
Cash, January 1, 2001		66,000
Cash, December 31, 2001		$ 84,000

*30,000 + 21,600 − 24,000

Schedule of Noncash Investing and Financing Activities:

Acquisition of land by issuance of common stock	$ 20,000

Problem 2

Stellar Inc.
Statement of Cash Flows
For Year Ended December 31, 2001

Cash flows from operating activities:		
Cash received from customers		$563,000
Deduct: Cash payments for merchandise	$211,800	
Cash payments for operating expenses	169,600	
Cash payments for income tax	34,000	415,400
Net cash flow from operating activities		$147,600
Cash flows from investing activities:		
Cash received from land sold	$ 54,000	
Less cash paid for purchase of equipment	96,000	
Net cash flow used for investing activities		(42,000)
Cash flows from financing activities:		
Cash used to retire bonds payable	$ 60,000	
Cash paid for dividends	27,600*	
Net cash flow used for financing activities		(87,600)
Increase in cash		$ 18,000
Cash, January 1, 2001		66,000
Cash, December 31, 2001		$ 84,000

*30,000 + 21,600 − 24,000

Schedule of Noncash Investing and Financing Activities:
Acquisition of land by issuance of common stock .... $ 20,000

Schedule Reconciling Net Income with Cash Flows from Operating Activities:

Net income, per income statement		$114,000
Add: Depreciation	$48,000	
Decrease in inventories	6,000	
Decrease in prepaid expenses	2,400	
Increase in accounts payable	7,200	63,600
		$177,600
Deduct: Increase in trade receivables	$12,000	
Gain on sale of land	18,000	30,000
Net cash flow provided by operating activities		$147,600

Supporting calculations:

Sales (reported on income statement)	$575,000
Less increase in trade receivables	(12,000)
Cash received	$563,000
Cost of merchandise sold	$225,000
Less decrease in inventories	(6,000)
Less increase in accounts payable	(7,200)
Cash payments for merchandise	$211,800
Operating expenses (other than depreciation)	$172,000
Less decrease in prepaid expenses	(2,400)
Cash payments for operating expenses	$169,600

FINANCIAL STATEMENT ANALYSIS

Fill In the Blank—Part A

1. vertical analysis
2. profitability analysis
3. current position analysis
4. solvency
5. common-size
6. current
7. net sales to assets
8. acid-test
9. earnings per share on common stock
10. working capital
11. accounts receivable turnover
12. inventory turnover
13. liabilities to stockholders' equity
14. preferred dividends are earned
15. income from operations
16. stockholders' equity
17. dividends
18. independent audit
19. fixed assets to long-term liabilities
20. net sales

Fill In the Blank—Part B

1. horizontal analysis
2. dividend yield
3. independent auditors'
4. number of days' sales in receivables
5. number of days' sales in inventory
6. interest charges earned
7. rate earned on total assets
8. rate earned on stockholders' equity
9. leverage
10. price-earnings
11. management report
12. quick assets
13. common-size
14. solvency analysis
15. bankers'
16. number of days' sales in inventory
17. earnings per share (on common stock)
18. common-size
19. receivables
20. management report

Multiple Choice

1. d	6. d
2. c	7. c
3. c	8. a
4. b	9. b
5. d	10. c

True/False

1. F	6. T
2. T	7. F
3. F	8. T
4. T	9. T
5. F	10. F

Exercise 1

	2000	Percent	1999	Percent
Revenues	$450,000	100%	$389,000	100%
Costs and expenses:				
Cost of sales	$200,000	44%	$176,000	45%
Selling and administrative expenses	100,000	23%	73,000	19%
Interest expense	250	0%	396	0%
Total costs and expenses	$300,250	67%	$249,396	64%
Earnings before income taxes	$149,750	33%	$139,604	36%
Income taxes	35,321	8%	33,765	9%
Net earnings	$114,429	25%	$105,839	27%

Exercise 2

			Increase (Decrease)	
	2000	1999	Amount	Percent
Current assets	$250,000	$219,500	$30,500	14%
Fixed assets	435,000	401,600	33,400	8%
Intangible assets	42,000	46,500	(4,500)	−10%
Current liabilities	88,000	80,000	8,000	10%
Long-term liabilities	225,000	250,000	(25,000)	−10%
Common stock	214,000	167,600	46,400	28%
Retained earnings	200,000	170,000	30,000	18%

Problem 1

Nordic Inc.
Comparative Income Statement
For the Years Ended December 31, 2000 and 1999

			Increase (Decrease)	
	2000	1999	Amount	Percent
Sales	$690,500	$585,000	$105,500	18.0%
Sales returns and allowances	25,500	23,000	2,500	10.9%
Net sales	$665,000	$562,000	$103,000	18.3%
Cost of goods sold	420,000	330,000	90,000	27.3%
Gross profit	$245,000	$232,000	$ 13,000	5.6%
Selling expenses	$ 43,000	$ 47,700	$ (4,700)	−9.9%
Administrative expenses	31,000	31,000	0	0.0%
Total operating expenses	$ 74,000	$ 78,700	$ (4,700)	−6.0%
Operating income	$171,000	$153,300	$ 17,700	11.5%
Other income	13,000	16,400	(3,400)	−20.7%
	$184,000	$169,700	$ 14,300	8.4%
Other expense	58,000	53,500	4,500	8.4%
Income before income taxes	$126,000	$116,200	$ 9,800	8.4%
Income taxes	34,000	32,400	1,600	4.9%
Net income	$ 92,000	$ 83,800	$ 8,200	9.8%

Nordic Inc.
Comparative Balance Sheet
December 31, 2000 and 1999

| | | | Increase (Decrease) | |
Assets	2000	1999	Amount	Percent
Cash	$ 76,000	$ 69,000	$ 7,000	10.1%
Marketable securities	98,900	130,000	(31,100)	−23.9%
Accounts receivable (net)	199,000	195,000	4,000	2.1%
Inventory	450,000	375,000	75,000	20.0%
Prepaid expenses	28,000	26,300	1,700	6.5%
Long-term investments	35,000	35,000	0	0.0%
Fixed assets (net)	871,000	835,000	36,000	4.3%
Intangible assets	18,000	22,800	(4,800)	−21.1%
Total assets	$1,775,900	$1,688,100	$87,800	5.2%
Liabilities				
Current liabilities	$ 129,000	$ 107,000	$22,000	20.6%
Long-term liabilities	420,000	440,000	(20,000)	−4.5%
Total liabilities	$ 549,000	$ 547,000	$ 2,000	0.4%
Stockholders' Equity				
Preferred 3% stock, $100 par	$ 102,000	$ 93,000	$ 9,000	9.7%
Common stock, $50 par	549,900	530,100	19,800	3.7%
Retained earnings	575,000	518,000	57,000	11.0%
Total stockholders' equity	$1,226,900	$1,141,100	$85,800	7.5%
Total liabilities and stockholders' equity	$1,775,900	$1,688,100	$87,800	5.2%

Problem 2

Voyageur Inc.
Comparative Balance Sheet
December 31, 2000 and 1999

| | 2000 | | 1999 | |
Assets	Amount	Percent	Amount	Percent
Cash	$ 500,000	5.3%	$ 425,000	5.4%
Marketable securities	200,000	2.1%	185,000	2.4%
Accounts receivable (net)	680,000	7.3%	575,000	7.3%
Inventory	860,000	9.2%	740,000	9.4%
Prepaid expenses	104,000	1.1%	95,000	1.2%
Long-term investments	450,000	4.8%	410,000	5.2%
Fixed assets (net)	6,556,000	70.1%	5,420,000	69.0%
Total assets	$9,350,000	100.0%	$7,850,000	100.0%
Liabilities				
Current liabilities	$1,090,000	11.7%	$1,050,000	13.4%
Long-term liabilities	2,150,000	23.0%	2,050,000	26.1%
Total liabilities	$3,240,000	34.7%	$3,100,000	39.5%
Stockholders' Equity				
Preferred 5% stock, $100 par	$ 350,000	3.7%	$ 350,000	4.5%
Common stock, $10 par	2,550,000	27.3%	2,550,000	32.5%
Retained earnings	3,210,000	34.3%	1,850,000	23.5%
Total stockholders' equity	$6,110,000	65.3%	$4,750,000	60.5%
Total liabilities and stockholders' equity	$9,350,000	100.0%	$7,850,000	100.0%

Voyageur Inc.
Income Statement
For the Year Ended December 31, 2000

	Amount	Percent
Sales	$12,800,000	102.4%
Sales returns and allowances	300,000	2.4%
Net sales	$12,500,000	100.0%
Cost of goods sold	7,550,000	60.4%
Gross profit	$ 4,950,000	39.6%
Selling expenses	$ 1,550,000	12.4%
Administrative expenses	825,000	6.6%
Total operating expenses	$ 2,375,000	19.0%
Operating income	$ 2,575,000	20.6%
Other income	125,000	1.0%
	$ 2,700,000	21.6%
Other expense (interest)	150,000	1.2%
Income before income taxes	$ 2,550,000	20.4%
Income taxes	937,000	7.5%
Net income	$ 1,613,000	12.9%

Problem 3

		Calculation	Final Result
a.	Working capital	$2,344,000 − $1,090,000	1,254,000
b.	Current ratio	$\dfrac{\$2,344,000}{\$1,090,000}$	2.2
c.	Acid-test ratio	$\dfrac{\$1,380,000}{\$1,090,000}$	1.3
d.	Accounts receivable turnover	$\dfrac{\$12,500,000}{\left(\dfrac{\$680,000+\$575,000}{2}\right)}$	19.9
e.	Number of days' sales in receivables	$\dfrac{\$12,500,000}{365}=\$34,247 \quad \dfrac{\$680,000}{\$34,247}$	19.9
f.	Inventory turnover	$\dfrac{\$7,550,000}{\left(\dfrac{\$860,000+\$740,000}{2}\right)}$	9.4
g.	Number of days' sales in inventory	$\dfrac{\$7,550,000}{365}=\$20,685 \quad \dfrac{\$860,000}{\$20,685}$	41.6
h.	Ratio of fixed assets to long-term liabilities	$\dfrac{\$6,556,000}{\$2,150,000}$	3.0
i.	Ratio of liabilities to stockholders' equity	$\dfrac{\$3,240,000}{\$6,110,000}$	0.5
j.	Number of times interest charges earned	$\dfrac{\$2,550,000+\$150,000}{\$150,000}$	18.0
k.	Number of times preferred dividends earned	$\dfrac{\$1,613,000}{\$17,500}$	92.2

		Calculation	Final Result
l.	Ratio of net sales to assets	$$\frac{\$12,500,000}{\left(\dfrac{\$8,900,000+\$7,440,000}{2}\right)}$$	1.5
m.	Rate earned on total assets	$$\frac{\$1,613,000+\$150,000}{\left(\dfrac{\$9,350,000+\$7,850,000}{2}\right)}$$	20.5%
n.	Rate earned on stockholders' equity	$$\frac{\$1,613,000}{\left(\dfrac{\$6,110,000+\$4,750,000}{2}\right)}$$	29.7%
o.	Rate earned on common stockholders' equity	$$\frac{\$1,613,000-\$17,500}{\left(\dfrac{\$5,760,000+\$4,400,000}{2}\right)}$$	31.4%
p.	Earnings per share on common stock	$$\frac{\$1,613,000-\$17,500}{255,000}$$	$6.26
q.	Price-earnings ratio	$$\frac{\$29.75}{\$6.26}$$	4.8
r.	Dividends per share of common stock	$$\frac{\$250,000}{255,000}$$	$.98
s.	Dividend yield	$$\frac{\left(\dfrac{\$250,000}{255,000 \text{ shares}}\right)}{\$29.75}$$	3.3%